Uncertain Accommodation

Law and Society Series
W. Wesley Pue, General Editor

The Law and Society Series explores law as a socially embedded phenomenon. It is premised on the understanding that the conventional division of law from society creates false dichotomies in thinking, scholarship, educational practice, and social life. Books in the series treat law and society as mutually constitutive and seek to bridge scholarship emerging from interdisciplinary engagement of law with disciplines such as politics, social theory, history, political economy, and gender studies.

A list of recent titles in the series appears at the end of the book. For a complete list, see the UBC Press website, www.ubcpress.ca/books/series_law.html.

Uncertain Accommodation

Aboriginal Identity and Group Rights in the Supreme Court of Canada

DIMITRIOS PANAGOS

UBCPress · Vancouver · Toronto

25 24 23 22 21 20 19 18 17 16   5 4 3 2 1

Printed in Canada on FSC-certified ancient-forest-free paper
(100% post-consumer recycled) that is processed chlorine- and acid-free.

Library and Archives Canada Cataloguing in Publication

Panagos, Dimitrios, author
Uncertain accommodation : aboriginal identity and group rights in
the Supreme Court of Canada / Dimitrios Panagos.

(Law and society series)
Includes bibliographical references and index.
Issued in print and electronic formats.
ISBN 978-0-7748-3239-7 (pbk.). –ISBN 978-0-7748-3240-3 (pdf). –
ISBN 978-0-7748-3241-0 (epub). – ISBN 978-0-7748-3328-8 (mobi)

1. Canada. Supreme Court.   2. Native peoples – Legal status, laws, etc. – Canada.   3. Native
peoples – Civil rights–Canada.   4. Native peoples – Canada – Ethnic identity.   5. Group
rights–Canada.   I. Title.   II. Series: Law and society series (Vancouver, B.C.)

KE7709.P38 2016	342.7108'72	C2016-904073-9
KF8205.P38 2016		C2016-904074-7

Canadä

UBC Press gratefully acknowledges the financial support for our
publishing program of the Government of Canada (through the Canada Book Fund),
the Canada Council for the Arts, and the British Columbia Arts Council.

This book has been published with the help of a grant from the
Canadian Federation for the Humanities and Social Sciences, through the
Awards to Scholarly Publications Program, using funds provided
by the Social Sciences and Humanities Research Council of Canada.

Printed and bound in Canada by Friesens
Set in Zurich, Univers and Minion by Marquis Interscript.
Copy editor: Katrina Petrik
Proofreader: Alison Strobel
Indexer: Judy Dunlop

UBC Press
The University of British Columbia
2029 West Mall
Vancouver, BC V6T 1Z2

www.ubcpress.ca

Contents

Acknowledgments

I would like to begin by thanking my family. The completion of this book was possible only as a result of the significant emotional and financial support provided by my parents, Elli and Peter; my sister, Iris; my brother-in-law, Steve; my niece, Elli, and nephew, Odysseas; and my best friend Niveanne. This book is dedicated to them.

I would like to thank Eleanor MacDonald. Eleanor has been my academic mentor, my advocate, and one of my most enthusiastic supporters. I could not have completed this book without her guidance and encouragement. I would also like to extend my gratitude to Joyce Green. Her thought-provoking questions, as well as her kind words of support over the years are very much appreciated.

The transition from manuscript to book is at times daunting and difficult. In my case, the transition was only possible as a result of the significant efforts of the people at UBC Press. Since the beginning of this journey, I have had the good fortune of working with Randy Schmidt. Over the years, Randy has impressed me with his seemingly boundless patience, his sage advice for navigating each stage of the publishing process, and his cutting sense of humour. I would also like to thank the two anonymous reviewers who commented on the manuscript; their suggestions were insightful. This book has certainly benefited from their participation in the peer-review process.

Thus far, I have had the great privilege of being a member of two fantastic academic communities, first as a doctoral student at Queen's University (Kingston) and now as a member of the Department of Political

Science at Memorial University (St. John's). I would like to thank the many students that have endured my lectures on political theory. Your efforts in my classes, your probing questions, your successes, and your enthusiasm push me to constantly strive to be a better teacher and scholar. You are a constant source of inspiration.

Over the years, friends and colleagues at Queen's University and Memorial University have been important sources of support and significant role models. This has been especially true of Mira Bachvarova, Keith Banting, Amanda Bittner, Elizabeth Goodyear-Grant, J. Andrew Grant, Anne G. Graham, Nicholas Hardy, Janet Hiebert, Margaret Moore, Allison McCulloch, Tamara Small, and Russell Williams.

Finally, I would like to thank J. Scott Matthews, who, in addition to reading and providing feedback on many chapters of the manuscript, has been a constant source of support and encouragement. He has done a significant amount of the "heavy lifting" on this score, and I am very grateful.

Uncertain Accommodation

Introduction

The phrase "identity-related differences" refers to those characteristics that define individuals as certain kinds of persons (or as members of certain kinds of groups). These characteristics can be acquired both voluntarily and involuntarily. Over two decades ago, political theorist Avigail Eisenberg (1994, 9) observed that the issue of "which identity-related characteristics are most significant will partly depend on what sort of characteristics have political significance within a community." We have increasingly become aware of the dangers of ignoring and over-emphasizing these differences. History is replete with instances of injustice originating in society's failure to adequately address diversity and difference and, even worse, its active attempts to eliminate certain identity-related differences entirely. We should be particularly concerned about how the state manages these differences – as opposed to other societal actors – because, as political theorist Jacob Levy (2000, 23) argues, the state "has an unparalleled capacity to act cruelly, to inflict violence and pain, to inspire fear." The unfortunate fate of many religious, national, and cultural groups, as well as sexual and racial minorities in this past century alone, stands as a powerful testament to the accuracy of Levy's argument. This historical record has contributed to a growing consensus among scholars that justice requires states to do better – that is, for states to be considered just (or at least reasonably so), they need to protect and accommodate identity groups within their borders (Gutmann 1994, 4–5; Kymlicka 1995).

So, what is to be done? How can states act justly? There are many possible answers to these questions. I would hazard that a number of these responses – perhaps even a majority – include something about rights. When I use the term "rights," I take it to mean what philosophers such as George W. Rainbolt (1993, 93) have in mind: that rights are properly conceptualized as normative constraints. To say that a person has a right, then, is to say that they have a claim to X (where X is usually understood as an important human interest or value such as physical security or personal expression) and everyone else has a sufficient reason to respect that person's claim.[1] If someone holds a right, this is a sufficient (though not conclusive) reason for everyone else to behave in a way that is compatible with that person's holding that right (i.e., usually by constraining his or her behaviour).[2] For example, if we say that a person has a right to associate with people of her choosing, the rest of us have a sufficient reason to allow this to occur (i.e., by not locking the person in her home or physically stopping her from getting together with people whom we dislike). Many of the standard civil and political rights in most liberal democratic states fit with this notion of rights as normative constraints.

My intuition about rights and the question of what states can do should not be too controversial given the important space we have carved out for rights in our contemporary world. Philosopher A. John Simmons (2008, 68) aptly explains this point by bringing to our attention the fact that rights are often thought to be important because people associate them with justice: "That there is a strong connection between the satisfaction of people's rights and the (modern) idea of justice seems indisputable, as can be seen in the agreement on this point by moral thinkers as diverse (in period and in orientation) as John Locke, Immanuel Kant, and John Stuart Mill." People expect rights to play a role in the pursuit of justice, and many philosophical heavyweights support this expectation, though for different reasons. The connection between justice and rights renders intelligible legal philosopher Jeremy Waldron's (2005, 109) somewhat sobering observation that in a world marked by conflict and hard choices, rights "are supposed to be our best, most honest, and most respectful response."

When this argument about rights and justice is applied to the relationship between states and identity groups, the claim is somewhat transformed. It becomes something like the following: Justice (at least sometimes) requires states to extend group rights to certain identity groups and to create institutional measures for the protection of these rights. I refer to "group" rights as those that go beyond the standard package of civil rights (e.g., the right to free expression or movement) and political rights (e.g., the right to vote or stand for office) accorded to citizens generally in contemporary liberal democracies. The distinguishing feature of group rights is that they are held by people (either individually or collectively) because they are members of certain identity groups, and their purpose is to ensure the well-being or survival of these groups. Some scholars object to the very idea of group rights, arguing that they are incompatible with the basic moral equality of citizens (Barry 2001). Others, however, present compelling philosophical cases for these rights. Arguably, the most well-known account is by Canadian political philosopher Will Kymlicka. For Kymlicka (1995), a liberal multiculturalist, the extension of group rights is legitimate if it facilitates individual autonomy. As political theorist Mira Bachvarova (2014, 4) observes, "Kymlicka's commitment to the value of personal autonomy led him to consider, more expansively than most liberals did, the conditions for the effective exercise of autonomy." Specifically, Kymlicka argues that autonomy is always exercised in a socio-cultural context (what he calls a "societal culture"), which makes individual choice both meaningful and possible.[3] This connection between autonomy and culture creates two problems for people who are not members of the majority cultural group – whom Kymlicka identifies as people who belong to polyethnic groups (e.g., immigrants and their descendants) and subnational minority groups (i.e., groups that are nations without their own states such as the Québécois or the Basque). The first problem is that members of minority groups may have a harder time operating in the societal culture of the majority. As a result, the extension of group rights can be an important resource to assist these individuals to navigate a societal culture that is not fully their own (Levey 1997, 216). The second problem is that the societal cultures of minority groups are at a disadvantage vis-à-vis their majority counterparts because the latter usually have more control over (or even exclusive access to) state institutions and resources. Thus, extending group rights to minorities can facilitate the autonomy of members of minority groups by protecting these groups' societal cultures. In both instances, group rights can create a degree of equality and fairness between people belonging to minority and majority groups.[4] On the whole, Kymlicka (1995) presents a robust and impressive argument that these rights can be legitimate tools for states to employ in their efforts to protect and accommodate minority groups, and his work continues to greatly influence many contemporary scholars and political practitioners.

Unfortunately, the move from theory to practice is seldom easy. This book is one account of what happened when, in the 1980s, the Canadian state made such a move and constitutionalized Aboriginal rights. It is not my intention to create the impression that the political authorities in Canada, moved by some sense of justice, acted to give Aboriginal rights constitutional recognition. In actuality, the 1982 adoption of the Aboriginal rights provision in the Canadian Constitution was the product of decades of mobilization by Aboriginal peoples and their allies (Manuel and Posluns 1974), as well as intense political bargaining between the federal government and the provincial premiers (Waddell 2003). The changes that came about in the early 1980s are thanks to these parties' hard work.

In 1982, the Canadian Constitution was amended substantially. The package of constitutional changes adopted included, among other measures, section 35, a provision recognizing Aboriginal and treaty rights. At the time, the adoption of section 35 was a very contentious matter. Indeed, it was so contentious that the only way for supporters of this provision to secure its ultimate inclusion in the constitutional package was for them to agree to leave it purposely vague. Essentially, the federal and provincial governments agreed to settle on a definition for section 35 at a series of first ministers' conferences to be held after the passage of the *Constitution Act, 1982*. The conferences failed to result in an agreement and, consequently, the Supreme Court of Canada (SCC) was left holding the metaphorical bag: It found itself with the task of outlining the nature and scope of section 35 and its corresponding rights.

The court's first opportunity to outline what Aboriginal rights would entail came about in the 1990 *Sparrow* decision.[5] Since then, a firestorm of criticism has ensued. For some scholars, Aboriginal rights go too far (Flanagan 2000); for others, they do not go far enough (Green 2000). Still others contend that Aboriginal rights are an important step toward Aboriginal-non-Aboriginal reconciliation in Canada (Cairns 2000), while their opponents insist that these rights are merely a continuation of the state's policies of assimilation and colonization (Alfred 2005). Interestingly, some scholars of Aboriginal politics view Canada's legal system in its entirety

– not just section 35 – as facilitating these state policies. Patricia Monture-Angus (1999), for example, argues that the legal system is an alien structure imposed on Aboriginal peoples that offers them very little in their struggle for self-determination. Moreover, all of these divergent scholarly opinions are reflected in the positions held by members of Aboriginal nations and communities, government officials, and the Canadian public at large. Legal scholar Jean Leclair (2006, 522) is correct in his assessment of the situation: "Since 1982, many people, from Supreme Court justices to legal scholars, be they aboriginal or non-aboriginal, have battled one another over the meaning that should be ascribed to the words 'aboriginal rights' found in section 35 of the *Constitution Act, 1982*." And yet, while very few are happy with the current state of Aboriginal rights in Canada, there is a lack of consensus about what is wrong with these rights and how to fix them.

As a non-Aboriginal Canadian and a scholar, I believe that this conflict is of great significance. It is of personal importance because I have a deep desire to be a citizen of a country that deals with all people who reside within its borders in a just fashion. This conflict is of scholarly importance because I am convinced that rights have an important role to play in treating people justly. However, given the degree of disagreement surrounding section 35, I think that it is proper to suspect that something has gone seriously wrong in this case. My goal in this book is to examine where the proverbial train went off the rails and, in so doing, participate in the conversation about how to get it back on track. This book focuses on the following questions: After so many years, why have Canadians been unable to reach any kind of consensus regarding where the SCC went wrong in its Aboriginal rights jurisprudence? More importantly for the future relationship between Aboriginal peoples and non-Aboriginal Canadians, why have Canadians been unable to agree on what Aboriginal rights should entail? And lastly, what does this Canadian case teach us about group rights, in terms of how they are theorized and how they can be put into practice?

Approach

Can the conflict over Aboriginal rights be resolved by altering, in some way, the scope of the rights covered by section 35? In other words, does the solution lie in extending the reach of these rights to cover additional Aboriginal interests (i.e., the position argued by Green 2000)? Or is the solution found by shrinking the reach of these rights to exclude certain matters (i.e., the position put forth by Flanagan 2000)? Characterizing the controversy surrounding section 35 as an issue of scope is one way – indeed a common way – of viewing the debate about these rights. This view underpins the claims of those who argue that Aboriginal rights go too far or do not go far enough.

Alternatively, one could ask whether the rights covered by section 35 suffer from some additional shortcoming that goes beyond issues of scope. That is, do other factors unrelated to scope play a significant role in the conflict? This book pursues this line of investigation. It does so as a result of the scholarly work put forward by those interested in the issue of identity, as well as those interested in how identity impacts rights. For decades, scholars have raised serious concerns about the use of the concept of identity in political analyses and prescriptions (Dhamoon 2009; Dick 2006). Rogers Brubaker and Frederick Cooper (2000, 2) go as far as arguing that the lack of academic consensus and precision over how to conceptualize identity renders this concept of little analytical value. They conclude that the analytical burden currently shouldered by identity can more effectively be borne by a bundle of other concepts. They argue that, in order to cover all of the issues and debates currently encompassed by the term "identity," we need three distinct concepts, not one: identification and categorization; self-understanding and social location; and commonality, connectedness, and groupness (Brubaker and Cooper 2000, 14–21).

The challenges associated with the use of the concept of identity give us reason, then, to doubt whether identity-based rights are the best mechanisms for protecting and accommodating identity groups such as Aboriginal nations. In this book, I explore this possibility. I do so, however, not by challenging the normative arguments advanced by scholars such as Kymlicka (1995) about the moral permissibility or optimality of these rights. Rather, I follow the lead of scholars such as Caroline Dick (2011) who focus on evaluating the performance of specific examples of these rights in action. I am interested in evaluating the degree to which section 35 rights protect and accommodate Aboriginal peoples in Canada (i.e., Dick's project), as opposed to the (philosophical) soundness of the normative case for group rights (i.e., Kymlicka's project).

This book begins by advancing that, while the scope of section 35 may, indeed, be a problem, problems may also result from the attempt to anchor section 35 rights to a particular group identity – in this case, aboriginality. Specifically, the conflict surrounding section 35 rights may be constituted by a debate about the scope of these rights, as well as a debate about the meaning of aboriginality. This book analyzes these two (possible) facets of the conflict by bringing together scholarship on Aboriginal politics, political philosophy, and the law. It evaluates judicial decisions, legal submissions (factums), and scholarly commentary pertaining to Aboriginal rights cases in Canada, with a focus on unpacking the roles competing conceptions of Aboriginal identity play in the construction and ultimate reception of section 35 rights.

This analysis demonstrates that, even though there are multiple conceptions of aboriginality – in other words, the Aboriginal litigants, the provinces, the federal government, and the Supreme Court justices advance different understandings of the collective identity – Aboriginal rights are constructed to protect a single, particular vision of aboriginality: the vision held by the justices of the SCC. This vision of aboriginality is quite different from the understanding of the collective identity put forward by the Aboriginal litigants themselves and challenges the litigants' version of aboriginality in important ways. This book advances the argument that, as a result of the SCC's actions, Aboriginal rights fail to protect Aboriginal peoples and even result in harm.

This central finding allows us to reframe and better comprehend the controversy surrounding Aboriginal rights in Canada. This book advances that, contrary to the traditional way of understanding the controversy, the contestation surrounding section 35 actually involves two related, yet separate disputes. One dispute – the dispute that is the standard focus of debate – is about the scope of the rights that Aboriginal peoples have or ought to have. The other dispute – the dispute that is often ignored – is about the very meaning of this collective identity. In order to accurately grasp the controversy surrounding section 35, both disputes need to be addressed.

The scoping dispute and the identity dispute are front and centre in this book's treatment of section 35 and are reflected in its prescriptions. Specifically, the book puts forward two recommendations as a result of the SCC's decision to tether section 35 rights to aboriginality. The first recommendation is that the proper way to settle the controversy over section 35 is to settle the debate over the meaning of aboriginality and, only then, to move on to establishing (or in this case, reconstructing) the scope of Aboriginal rights. That is, we need to decide what aboriginality means before we can come up with the right set of rights for its protection.

The second recommendation put forward in this book is that, as long as the SCC continues to insist on a connection between section 35 and aboriginality, the best way to settle the identity dispute is for Aboriginal rights to be based on Aboriginal peoples' understanding of aboriginality. The crux of the argument is that if group rights are anchored to a specific identity, then it is unfair to require members of the identity group to conform to an outsider's version of their identity as a condition of exercising these rights – especially if the group members did not agree to the link between rights and identity in the first place and this requirement has not been adequately justified to them. This is no way to treat people justly.

The book concludes with one additional observation. The analysis presented throughout problematizes the court's decision to tie Aboriginal rights to aboriginality. One is left wondering whether other interests not based on identity might be a sounder basis for Aboriginal rights in Canada. This is an important question moving forward. While this book does not provide an adequate, stand-alone case for separating group rights and identity given the problems that result from the connection in this Canadian case, it could be of use to those currently engaged in advancing such an argument.

Terminology

In her work on colonialism and resistance, Emma LaRocque (2010, 6) rightly cautions that "terminology about identities is a minefield." Thus, I offer the following explanation regarding my decision to use the term "Aboriginal." I recognize that a number of scholars have argued that this term is problematic. Some scholars argue that this term obscures the great diversity of communities and nations encompassed by this label – that it has a homogenizing effect (Vermette 2008, 7). Others contend that this label is the creation of those who do not bear this collective identity – that it is the white man's term (Dodson 1994). As one member of the Dene Nation put it: "Geez, first I was [an] Indian, then a Loucheux, then I had to call myself a Gwich'in, now I'm a First Nation – what the hell they gonna make me call myself next!?" (Irlbacher-Fox 2009, 35). And, of course, the term "Aboriginal" is not generally used by the individuals who are called "Aboriginal" (Wood 2003, 371–72). As Native American studies scholar Dale Turner (2006, 32) explains, "the primary source of identification for many Aboriginal peoples is their community, or nation. If you ask an indigenous person in North America where they are from, most will tell you their indigenous nation first: Mohawk, Lakota Sioux, Haida, Metis, to name a few." In short, these individuals have their own ways of referring to their nations that come from their own cultures and languages. In this book, the use of the term "Aboriginal" is not meant as an evaluative statement about the validity or significance of these issues or the corresponding academic scholarship. I am very sympathetic to these positions and believe that many of the arguments underpinning them are quite convincing. I have selected to use the term "Aboriginal" instead of other possible terms because it is the term employed in the *Constitution Act, 1982*. It is also the term employed in many of the legal documents that are the focus of the book's analysis (e.g., the judicial decisions and factums). And this term seems to be the term most often used in the scholarly literature on section 35. The term "Aboriginal" is selected in order to ensure a certain degree of coherence and clarity for the reader, especially the reader who is unfamiliar with the scholarship on Aboriginal politics and Canadian law.

Structure of the Book

The structure of the book allows readers a variety of ways of approaching the text. Chapter 1 provides historical context for the analysis that follows. Those whose primary interest is the law may want to focus their attention on Chapters 2, 6, and 7, which contain the bulk of the legal analysis in this book. Those whose primary interest is the politics of identity can jump to Chapters 3, 4, and 5, which focus on the nature of the contestation surrounding the meaning of aboriginality and possible approaches to defining this collective identity. Chapter 8 brings together the legal analyses and discussions about identity politics in order to advance the major conclusions of the book. Of course, like many who labour to produce a book, I hope that there is enough of interest here to encourage all readers, regardless of their expertise, to engage with the text as a whole. The contents of each chapter are outlined in more detail below.

Chapter 1 focuses on section 35, its history, and its current form. The first part of the chapter outlines the historical origins of the Aboriginal rights provision. The main objective of this historical presentation is to highlight that from the very beginning, there was fierce debate about what a constitutional provision recognizing Aboriginal rights should entail. The latter part of the chapter advances that the SCC was ultimately called upon to settle the debate regarding the nature and scope of section 35, and it decided that Aboriginal rights would be principally about protecting aboriginality.

Chapters 2, 3, and 4 focus on aboriginality. They illustrate that there are many ways to understand the term "Aboriginal" and to approach the conceptualization of aboriginality. Chapter 2 advances that the different possible meanings of aboriginality are, to an important degree, products of the different approaches that can be employed to conceptualize the collective identity. The chapter examines two of these approaches: the traits-based approach and the relational approach. Chapter 3 presents a critical comparison of the two approaches and makes the case for the use of the relational approach. The crux of the argument is that traits-based approaches manifest costs that are "weightier" than the costs associated with the relational approach, because they include real-world costs that affect people's lives. Chapter 4 employs a relational approach to construct three definitions of aboriginality by drawing on the literature on Aboriginal politics. I label these different versions of aboriginality the nation-to-nation, colonial, and citizen-state understandings of aboriginality. These three versions of aboriginality act as "ideal types" for my analysis of the court material in the two chapters that follow.

Chapter 5 turns back to the jurisprudence on section 35. The analysis focuses on the legal arguments submitted to the SCC by the Aboriginal, federal, and provincial participants in Aboriginal rights cases. The analysis demonstrates that the Aboriginal participants consistently advance one understanding of aboriginality (the nation-to-nation version), while the federal and provincial participants put forward two alternatives (the colonial and citizen-state versions). Chapter 6 also focuses on the court material, but specifically on the judicial decisions. What is of interest in this chapter is the version of aboriginality put forward by the justices of the SCC. During section 35 litigation, the justices invented and then consistently put forward the citizen-state understanding of aboriginality.

Chapters 7 and 8 illustrate the serious consequences of anchoring section 35 rights to the citizen-state understanding of aboriginality. Chapter 7 makes the case that section 35 rights cannot, in principle, protect all three versions of aboriginality. Specifically, the colonial and nation-to-nation conceptions do not receive protection. I conclude that, while an absence of protection for the colonial version of the collective identity is something worth celebrating (or so I argue), absence of protection for the nation-to-nation conception of aboriginality is worrisome. Chapter 8 presents the case for this last point in detail. Specifically, I argue that the court's decision to protect the citizen-state conception of aboriginality is not justified and harms Aboriginal peoples in two basic ways – it misrecognizes them and treats them unfairly. I put forward the proposal that section 35 rights should be reconstructed to protect the version of aboriginality held by the bearers of this collective identity. This is the only fair course of action, if the court insists on maintaining the linkage between Aboriginal rights and aboriginality.

1

The Historical and Legal Framework for Section 35

Prior to 1982, in Canada, the federal government and many provincial governments, as well as many non-Aboriginal Canadians, questioned the very idea of Aboriginal rights. Debates during the pre-1982 period were rarely about the nature or scope of Aboriginal rights but were, instead, often about whether these rights existed at all. According to Dale Turner (2006, 34–35), the denial of the existence of Aboriginal rights was made possible by the dominant discourse structuring Aboriginal-non-Aboriginal relations at the time. Turner contends that this discourse was underpinned by four interlocking beliefs held by non-Aboriginal Canadians: that Aboriginal-specific policies were discriminatory; that all Canadians should have exactly the same legal and political status; that treaties should be abandoned; and that mainstream society should do a better (more complete) job of assimilating Aboriginal peoples. Turner (2006, 34–35) evocatively refers to this set of claims as the "white orthodoxy." For Turner, the white orthodoxy goes a long way to explaining how it was possible for non-Aboriginal Canadians to deny the existence of Aboriginal rights for the better part of a century.

For supporters of the position that Aboriginal rights did indeed exist, the pre-1982 jurisprudence on these rights offered very little aid. The leading legal precedent, established in 1888, characterized Aboriginal rights as usufructs by declaring that "the tenure of the Indians was a personal and usufructuary right, dependent upon the good will of the Sovereign."[1] In order to fully grasp the significance of this legal precedent, it is important to understand what is meant by the term "usufruct." A usufruct is an ancient and specific right to the beneficial use of property. Legal scholar Herbert

Jolowicz (1967, quoted in Goldie 1985) characterizes it thus: "Usufruct is the right of using and taking the fruits of property belonging to another ... without the right of destroying or changing the character of the thing, and lasting only so long as the character remains unchanged." Ultimately, this Aboriginal-rights-as-usufruct view meant that, even though some Aboriginal peoples used and benefited from their traditional lands, as far as Canadian law was concerned, these lands actually belonged to another party (usually the Crown). Moreover, Aboriginal peoples' beneficial use rights to these lands could be brought to an end at any time by the non-Aboriginal owner. This view of Aboriginal rights remained in effect for almost one hundred years.

In 1973, the judicial reasons handed down in the case of *Calder et al. v. the Attorney-General of British Columbia* cast doubt on the Aboriginal-rights-as-usufructs view.[2] The Aboriginal appellants had sought a declaration that their title to one thousand square miles of traditional territory in northwestern British Columbia had not been (lawfully) extinguished. Even though the Aboriginal plaintiffs in the *Calder* case technically lost, a majority of the SCC justices recognized an Aboriginal right to land in their written reasons.[3] In addition, while the judges did not agree about whether the Aboriginal plaintiffs' rights existed at the time of litigation, half of them advanced that these rights (when they did exist) were more than mere usufructs (Harris 2009, 144). One important result of the *Calder* case was that it led to the establishment of the modern land claims process (Russell 2004, 94) – a significant shift in the legal landscape for Aboriginal rights in Canada. And yet, the period between 1973 and 1982 represents somewhat of a legal paradox. As legal scholar Peter Hogg (2009, 4) explains, on the one hand, the common law during that time recognized the existence of Aboriginal rights, but, on the other hand, the Canadian Constitution afforded these rights almost no protection.

In the early 1980s, Aboriginal rights (finally) received recognition in Canada's written constitution in section 35 of the *Constitution Act, 1982*. Section 35 is composed of four subsections; subsection (1) is the main focus of this book.

> (1) The existing aboriginal and treaty rights of the aboriginal peoples of Canada are hereby recognized and affirmed.

(2) In this Act, "aboriginal peoples of Canada" includes the Indian, Inuit and Metis peoples of Canada.

(3) For greater certainty, in subsection (1) "treaty rights" includes rights that now exist by way of land claims agreements or may be so acquired.

(4) Notwithstanding any other provision of this Act, the aboriginal and treaty rights referred to in subsection (1) are guaranteed equally to male and female persons.[4]

The "story" of the constitutionalization of Aboriginal rights has been traditionally told in two ways, and important differences mark the narratives depending on who does the telling. One narrative – advanced mostly by scholars of Canadian politics – presents the constitutionalization of these rights as one (important) facet of the persistent and seemingly intractable conflicts over constitutional reform that characterized Canadian politics in the latter half of the twentieth century. From this view, the constitutional recognition of Aboriginal rights, like so many other developments during this period (e.g., official bilingualism or the adoption of a bill of rights), was the product of the mega-constitutional politics of the day. Accordingly, political scientist Peter Russell contends that the constitutional wrangling of the time created important political possibilities for Aboriginal peoples. Russell (2004, 94) argues that "opening up both the substance and process of constitutional politics would eventually provide opportunity for Aboriginal peoples to assert their right to consent to the conditions on which they might be part of the Canadian community." He goes so far as to conclude that "it is unlikely that such an opportunity would have occurred had Canada's constitutional debate not addressed fundamental questions about the nature of the country and kept those questions open for so long" (Russell 2004, 94–95). A fair criticism of this narrative of the origins of section 35 is that its focus on reforming the Canadian Constitution risks reducing Aboriginal peoples to just one of many stakeholder groups struggling to secure their rights during this period (e.g., women's groups, minority francophone and anglophone communities, and visible minority groups). It pushes to the background the unique set of issues at the centre of the Aboriginal-non-Aboriginal conflict in Canada.

The alternative narrative – generally put forward by scholars of Aboriginal politics – avoids lumping the participants in the process of constitutional renewal into one category by advancing a different interpretation of the constitutionalization of Aboriginal rights. From this alternative view, the recognition of Aboriginal rights in the Canadian Constitution is one episode in the ongoing struggle between Aboriginal nations and the Canadian state (Cardinal 1999; Manuel 2003). For proponents of this view, the constitutionalization of Aboriginal rights marked the culmination of years of social mobilization on the part of Aboriginal communities and organizations. A number of Aboriginal scholars and political activists have outlined the hard-fought (and ultimately successful) battle by Aboriginal peoples to ensure the inclusion of an Aboriginal rights provision in the *Constitution Act, 1982* (Hawkes 1989; Poplar 2003; Miller 2004, 80–84). While many people expressed their disappointment with the final wording of subsection (1) of the provision, the important point is that in this narrative, Aboriginal peoples are at the heart of the events surrounding the constitutionalization of Aboriginal rights.

Regardless of the interpretive approach employed (and I do not offer any more comments on the issue here), a degree of familiarity with the sequence of events leading up to the constitutionalization of these rights is important for the analysis that follows. My immediate aim is to highlight two things: first, an Aboriginal rights provision was not included when the federal government and the provinces began the negotiations that ultimately led to the changes adopted in the *Constitution Act, 1982*; and second, the inclusion of the Aboriginal rights provision could only be achieved as a result of concessions to the provinces regarding its legal wording and exact meaning. In terms of the legal wording, the modifier "existing" was added before the words "aboriginal and treaty rights." And it was decided that the exact meaning of section 35 – the question of what this provision would entail – would be determined at a series of constitutionally mandated meetings to be held *after* the *Constitution Act, 1982*, became the law of the land.

For those unfamiliar with Canadian constitutional history, one important fact is likely to stand out: Prior to 1982, the British Parliament had to approve all amendments to the Canadian Constitution. When the federal government wanted to legislate on public policy issues that required a constitutional amendment, the British Parliament had to be involved. By the early part of the twentieth century, the British Parliament had developed a convention of passing these amendments without question or debate, thereby limiting the British Parliament's effect on the sovereignty of its Canadian counterpart (Chambers 1998, 146). Even so, when the Canadian government wanted to enact legislation on unemployment insurance and old age security pensions, it had to request that Westminster take the appropriate legislative steps to amend the Canadian Constitution and then wait for British parliamentarians to act.[5] This process was a holdover from the colonial period and, from at least the 1960s, was an important factor behind the call to "bring the Canadian Constitution home."[6] In order to shed this legal vestige of Canada's colonial past, the federal government and the provinces would need to patriate the Canadian Constitution; that is, to transfer authority from the British Parliament to the Canadian federal and provincial governments.

The Constitution would not be patriated, however, until 1982 when the federal and provincial governments (except Quebec) agreed on a set of constitutional amendments. The package of constitutional changes ultimately adopted went far beyond simply eliminating a role for the British Parliament in Canada's constitutional affairs. The package included, among other measures, a bill of rights (the *Canadian Charter of Rights and Freedoms*), a formula for all future constitutional amendments, guarantees regarding provincial fiscal equalization and, most importantly for our purposes here, a provision recognizing Aboriginal and treaty rights (section 35). It is not at all a stretch to say that the *Constitution Act, 1982*, is without parallel in terms of its impact on Canadian politics in the twentieth century.

The road to patriation was long and bumpy. Attempts by the federal and provincial governments to craft a mutually acceptable package of constitutional reforms began in the 1960s (Russell 2004, 3). And it took two decades of talks before the federal and provincial authorities first included an Aboriginal rights provision in these proposed changes. The first version of the Aboriginal rights provision appeared in the proposed package of amendments in April 1981 (Hogg 2009, 5). An early version of this provision read: "The aboriginal and treaty rights of the aboriginal peoples of Canada, as finally determined from time to time by the courts, are hereby recognized and affirmed" (Walkem and Bruce 2003, 7).

Then, in early November 1981, the Aboriginal rights provision was removed (Hogg 2009, 5). This was done, some scholars argue, in an effort to secure the support of certain provinces for the proposed constitutional changes. Scholars contend that some provincial representatives were concerned about the possible (negative) impact of an Aboriginal rights provision on provincial control over Crown lands and natural resources (Hawkes 1989, 6; Murphy 2006, 164). In late November, after intense lobbying efforts by Aboriginal activists, the Aboriginal rights provision was reinstated. However, the language of the proposed provision was altered and, among other changes, the modifier "existing" was added before the words "aboriginal and treaty rights" (Hawkes 1989, 6). Some people – especially the representatives of Aboriginal nations and organizations – worried that the modifier "existing" would make Aboriginal rights meaningless by leaving them open to legislative extinguishment (Poplar 2003, 26; Hogg 2009, 6). As a result of this wording, most of the national organizations representing Aboriginal peoples, including the Assembly of First Nations (AFN), did not endorse the final version of the package of constitutional reforms (Russell 2004, 122). Nevertheless, the *Constitution Act, 1982*, became law, and Aboriginal rights are now included in Canada's constitution.

Even though Aboriginal rights received recognition in the Constitution in 1982, the meaning of these rights was not yet settled. Indeed, Canadians would remain in the dark about the nature and scope of Aboriginal rights until the 1990s. Four conferences took place between 1983 and 1987, with participation from the seventeen official parties to the negotiations, including the federal and provincial governments, as well as some of the major Aboriginal organizations of the period (Hawkes 1989, 1). Settling on a meaning for section 35, however, proved to be a difficult task.[7] Aboriginal representatives maintained that the principle of self-determination ought to anchor section 35 and that the provision should protect the rights to Aboriginal self-government and Aboriginal title (Little Bear, Boldt, and Long 1984, 172–74; Walkem and Bruce 2003, 11). Numerous federal and provincial representatives put forward that stability and continuity should anchor section 35 and that the rights that came out of this provision should be primarily symbolic, upsetting the existing Canadian legal and political orders as little as possible (Asch 1999, 433).

Justice Binnie (1990, 240) – writing before his appointment to the SCC – explains how these diametrically opposed positions contributed to the failure of the constitutional negotiations: "For a variety of reasons, Aboriginal leaders in the constitutional talks insisted that the federal and provincial governments acknowledge an unqualified and undefined section 35 right to self-government. This, paradoxically, made it politically possible (if morally uninspiring) for the federal and provincial governments to walk away from the process and conveniently blame the failure on 'radical' native leaders." Whether it was due to a genuine inability to bridge the vast gulf that separated these competing positions or political gamesmanship, the four constitutional conferences failed to produce an agreement. As a consequence, the courts were left with the task of defining section 35. This fact makes the jurisprudence on this provision of singular importance if one aims to understand the nature and scope of constitutionally recognized Aboriginal rights in Canada.

Before proceeding with an analysis of the jurisprudence on this provision, a word about the scope of the examination contained in this book is required. Even though two types of rights (i.e., Aboriginal rights and treaty rights) are identified in section 35, these rights are very different; thus, their legal analyses are not interchangeable. This irreducibility is a product of their distinctive origins. Aboriginal traditions and customary laws are the source of Aboriginal rights, while treaty rights arise from the various treaties and treaty-like agreements concluded between Aboriginal nations and the Crown (both in its Euro-historical and contemporary, Canadian manifestations).[8] As a result of these distinctive origins, the principles that are employed in the legal interpretation of Aboriginal and treaty rights differ. This book follows legal scholar James Youngblood Henderson's (1997) advice to treat them differently and, as a consequence, deals almost exclusively with Aboriginal rights.

An analysis of the jurisprudence on Aboriginal rights begins with SCC rulings of the 1990s, when the court started handing down decisions on section 35 cases. In ruling on these cases, the SCC filled in a meaning for section 35. Given the intense disagreements during the constitutionally mandated conferences of the 1980s, an important question arises: Do Aboriginal rights as defined by the SCC coincide with the position taken by the Aboriginal participants or the government representatives? Stated differently, are Aboriginal rights about self-determination or are they mostly symbolic? An examination of section 35 jurisprudence reveals the position advanced by the SCC and the significant degree to which its position departs from both self-determination and symbolic recognition.

The SCC's Concern with Protecting Aboriginality

In 1990, the *Sparrow* case came before the SCC. This case, which involved the question of whether regulations managing the salmon fishery in British Columbia infringed on the Musqueam First Nation's Aboriginal rights, provided the court with its first opportunity to outline the nature and scope of section 35. The *Sparrow* decision began as follows: "This appeal requires this Court to explore for the first time the scope of section 35(1) of the *Constitution Act, 1982*, and to indicate its strength as a promise to the aboriginal peoples of Canada."[9] The court's reasoning in subsequent parts of the decision illustrated that the aforementioned "promise" was, in effect, a promise of accommodation.

To begin with, the SCC based a significant portion of its analysis in *Sparrow* on what it identified as the purposes underlying the inclusion of section 35 in the *Constitution Act, 1982*. The court stated that "the context of 1982 is surely enough to tell us that this is not just a codification of the case law on aboriginal rights that had accumulated by 1982. Section 35 calls for a just settlement for aboriginal peoples."[10] Put differently, this provision was not meant to constitutionalize the existing state of affairs between Aboriginal peoples and the Crown. Instead, it was meant to signal a change in the status quo – a change that would, according to the court, bring about a "just settlement." This was an explicit rejection of the position advanced by many of the government representatives during the constitutional meetings of the 1980s. Aboriginal rights would be more than mere symbolism. However, would they be about self-determination, as the Aboriginal representatives hoped? The answer to this question is found in what the SCC said about the boundaries of this just settlement and the intended purpose of section 35. The SCC explained that

> while [section 35] does not promise immunity from government regu-
> lation in a society that, in the twentieth century, is increasingly more
> complex, interdependent and sophisticated, and where exhaustible

resources need protection and management, it does hold the Crown to a substantive promise. The government is required to bear the burden of justifying any legislation that has some negative effect on any aboriginal rights protected under s. 35(1).[11]

Factors including development, economic considerations, interdependency, and the like were offered by the court as reasons to explain the absence of a constitutional guarantee of immunity from government regulation.[12] Consequently, the manner in which the Crown may exercise its power was altered (a result of the necessity to justify legislation that infringes on rights covered by this constitutional provision), but the ultimate scope of the Crown's power remained fundamentally unchanged. This, then, is the just settlement envisioned by the SCC; this is the strength of the promise mentioned in *Sparrow*. The court envisioned an alteration of the existing relations between the Crown and Aboriginal peoples, rather than a complete transformation of these relations. In other words, the just settlement in *Sparrow* involved some kind of accommodation, not overarching legal and political change.

A question follows from this last point: What exactly did the court envision was being accommodated by section 35? Six years after *Sparrow*, the *Van der Peet* case provided the SCC with the opportunity to address this question.[13] The case involved the question of whether a member of the Stó:lō First Nation of British Columbia had an Aboriginal right to sell salmon in contravention of existing fishing regulations. Writing for the majority, Chief Justice Lamer explained that Aboriginal rights "arise from the fact that aboriginal people are aboriginal" and "inhere in the very meaning of aboriginality."[14] Chief Justice Lamer reasoned that the court must "define aboriginal rights in a manner which recognizes that aboriginal rights are rights but which does so without losing sight of the fact that they are rights held by aboriginal peoples because they are aboriginal."[15] He insisted that the "Court must define the scope of s. 35(1) in a way which captures both the aboriginal and the rights in aboriginal rights."[16] Chief Justice Lamer argued that proceeding along these lines revealed that Aboriginal rights were constitutionalized in order to reconcile the Crown's sovereignty with one fundamental historical fact: "When Europeans arrived in North America, aboriginal peoples were already here, living in communities on the land, and participating in distinctive culture, as they had done for centuries."[17] For the SCC, pre-existing Aboriginal cultures in North America at the time of contact form the "basis for the special status that aboriginal peoples have within Canadian society"[18] – that is, the existence of pre-contact Aboriginal cultures is the reason why Aboriginal Canadians have rights that are not available to any other (i.e., non-Aboriginal) Canadian citizen.

In the *Van der Peet* decision, Chief Justice Lamer outlined the close relationship between section 35 rights and aboriginality. Aboriginal rights are intimately linked with aboriginality in that they owe their genesis to the existence of the collective identity. Moreover, the question of who may hold and exercise these rights is settled by identity-related considerations. Lastly, and most significantly, these rights are portrayed as aiming to accommodate the bearers of the collective identity through the reconciliation of their distinctive cultures with non-Aboriginal society. And this reconciliation is created by protecting aboriginality – by finding ways to mitigate the adverse effects of the Canadian legal and political orders.

What was missing from the SCC's rationale for Aboriginal rights as described in the *Van der Peet* decision was any mention of the fact that Aboriginal peoples are (or should be) self-determining. Also missing was anything substantive about the need to protect or accommodate Aboriginal legal and political orders. In short, the SCC's rationale for Aboriginal rights included nothing that comes close to the position advanced by the Aboriginal representatives during the constitutional meetings of the 1980s. Thus, in the end, the Aboriginal representatives did no better than their government counterparts in convincing the SCC to adopt their views about what section 35 ought to entail. The court decided to chart its own course: namely, it decided that section 35 rights would be about accommodating Aboriginal peoples by protecting aboriginality.

The Legal Tests for Section 35

In the *Sparrow* and *Van der Peet* decisions, the SCC not only identified the purpose for including section 35 in the *Constitution Act, 1982*, it also spelled out the requisite legal tests for pursuing an Aboriginal rights claim in Canada. The following analysis of the legal tests for activity-based and territorial claims – the two main types of section 35 rights claims identified by the court – is not intended to be a "how-to" guide for successfully executing a section 35 claim. Rather, I use it to illustrate the numerous ways in which the court embedded identity-related considerations into these legal tests. My ultimate aim is to demonstrate the significant degree to which section 35 rights are fashioned to protect aboriginality.

In the *Sparrow* decision, the SCC put forward that three principal questions structure the legal framework for section 35 activity-based claims. First, is there an existing Aboriginal right? Second, has there been a prima facie infringement of that right? And third, has the infringement been justified by the Crown? (Stevenson 2003) The Aboriginal rights–claimants are responsible for building the case that the answers to the first two questions are affirmative – that is, that a section 35 right exists and has been infringed. The Crown is responsible for making the argument that the answer to the third question is affirmative – that is, that the section 35 right at issue was lawfully infringed.

To address the first question, regarding whether an Aboriginal right exists, the *Van der Peet* decision developed a three-step process for identifying an existing activity-based Aboriginal right. The first step entails a characterization of the right being claimed. In order to qualify as an Aboriginal right of this type, the claim must centre on an Aboriginal practice, custom, or tradition.[19] Identifiable practices hold a significant place in the court's construction of activity-based Aboriginal rights. Among other things, practices provide the necessary link between section 35 rights and the protection of Aboriginal culture and societies. The SCC has gone so far as to characterize practices as requisite triggers for section 35 protection. This is clearly evident in the case of *R. v. Sappier; R. v. Gray,* in which the SCC put forward the following:

> The goal for courts is, therefore, to determine how the claimed right relates to the pre-contact culture or way of life of an aboriginal society. This has been achieved by requiring aboriginal rights–claimants to found their claim on a pre-contact practice which was integral to the distinctive culture of an aboriginal community. It is crucially important that the Court be able to identify a *practice* that helps to define the distinctive way of life of the aboriginal community as an aboriginal community. The importance of leading evidence about the pre-contact practice upon

which the claimed right is based should not be understated. In the absence of such evidence, courts will find it difficult to relate the claimed right to the pre-contact way of life of the specific aboriginal group, so as to trigger s. 35 protection.[20]

In short, an inability to identify an appropriate practice can translate into a failure to get a section 35 activity-based claim off the ground.

The second step to establishing the existence of an activity-based section 35 right consists of settling whether the practice, custom, or tradition is integral to the distinctive culture of an Aboriginal group.[21] Here, the most important terms are "distinctive" and "integral." First, "distinctive" does not mean unique. As the court clearly stated in the *Van der Peet* decision, a "distinctive" practice, custom, or tradition should be understood as "distinguishing" or "characteristic."[22] Second, the term "integral" means that the practice, custom, or tradition must not be merely incidental to a pre-contact Aboriginal culture but must be centrally important to that culture.[23] This means that a practice, custom, or tradition that is generally present in many or most human societies would not qualify. The court cited the eating of food in order to survive as an example of a general practice, custom, or tradition that could not be the basis for an Aboriginal right.[24]

The final step in identifying an existing activity-based Aboriginal right requires demonstrating that the practice, custom, or tradition originated in the pre-contact period or, in the case of the Metis, in the period up to the point when the Crown established effective control.[25] This temporal requirement is supplemented by what has been called the "principle of continuity," which holds that it is necessary to demonstrate that the practice, custom, or tradition existed both prior to contact with Europeans (or when the Crown established control over a particular area) and continued to exist in some shape or form forward through time. As a consequence, practices, customs and traditions that resulted solely from contact with Europeans cannot be the basis of an Aboriginal right.[26] While practices, customs, and traditions whose genesis was solely contingent on interactions with Europeans do not constitute a proper basis for an activity-based Aboriginal right, the principle of continuity makes some headway in ensuring that post-contact considerations play a role in the process of rights identification. As legal scholar Kent McNeil (2004a, 134) explains, "the concept of continuity ... serves the purpose of lessening the burden of proof of Aboriginal rights by allowing Aboriginal claimants to use post-contact practices, customs, and traditions to prove the pre-contact practices, customs, and traditions necessary to establish Aboriginal rights." Consequently, even though post-contact practices, customs, and traditions cannot be the basis of an Aboriginal right, they may be employed to establish a link to practices, customs, and traditions of the requisite periods. Thus, post-contact (or post-control) practices, customs, and traditions are not entirely irrelevant to the process of identifying an activity-based Aboriginal right.

With respect to the principle of continuity, the Aboriginal claimants must not only demonstrate that the right in question finds its source in the appropriate period, but they must also prove that it was not extinguished through surrender (through a historical or modern treaty) or by a constitutionally competent legislative body (McNeil 2004a, 134–35). The SCC has established that the federal Crown can extinguish an Aboriginal right by including a plain and clear statement of extinguishment in legislation.[27] And in the *Sappier; Gray* decision, the court clarified that the "plain and clear" requirement can be satisfied by both explicit and implicit Crown intent.[28]

Once the Aboriginal plaintiffs have successfully demonstrated that an activity-based Aboriginal right exists, they must address whether they have suffered some sort of infringement of that right. Specifically, the Aboriginal plaintiffs must illustrate that there is a prima facie case that the section 35 right at issue has been unlawfully breached. Making a prima facie case basically means that one of the parties in a case is required to produce evidence of a certain type – the court determines in advance what sort of evidence is sufficient – that is accepted as an adequate basis for advancing a particular legal inference. The court has stated that Aboriginal plaintiffs can successfully establish a prima facie case that a section 35 right has been infringed if they can produce evidence illustrating one of the following: that the offending legislation, regulation, or the like is (1) unreasonable; (2) imposes undue hardships on the Aboriginal group; or (3) denies a preferred means of exercising an Aboriginal right.[29]

In regard to the third question to test the pursuit of an activity-based Aboriginal rights claim – whether infringement has been justified by the Crown – the Crown may attempt to demonstrate that an infringement of an Aboriginal right is lawful. The Crown can accomplish this through a two-part process. The first part of the process hinges on whether a valid objective underpins the legislation in question.[30] In this instance, a valid legislative objective is one that is sensitive to both the historical facts of Aboriginal occupation and pre-contact (or, in the case of the Metis, pre-control) cultures and the reconciliation of these facts with the sovereignty of the Crown (Stevenson 2003, 70). According to the SCC, the development of agriculture, forestry, and mining, the building of infrastructure, and other considerations constitute valid reasons for the Crown to act in a fashion that infringes on Aboriginal rights.[31] According to legal scholar Mark Stevenson (2003, 71), the breadth of this list makes the threshold for a valid legislative object relatively easy for the Crown to meet, and this leads him to conclude that this stage of the process for justifying the infringement of an Aboriginal right is tilted in the Crown's favour. However, developments over the past decade or so in the jurisprudence on the Crown's duty to consult and accommodate Aboriginal peoples have certainly increased this threshold. I outline these developments below.

Once the Crown has demonstrated that a valid legislative objective exists, it must then demonstrate that the legislation in question does not breach its fiduciary relationship with Aboriginal peoples.[32] In common parlance, a fiduciary relationship usually means a legal relationship in which one person is partially or entirely responsible for another person and/or his property. In law, many relationships of responsibility are covered by the law of trusts, and this can lead to significant confusion between fiduciary relationships and trusts (Sealy 1962, 72). According to legal scholar L.S. Sealy (1962, 72), the term fiduciary is "more precisely used, in *contrast* with trusts proper, in reference to those situations which are in *some* respects trustlike, but are not strictly speaking trusts." And this distinction seems to be what the court intended when it began discussing in detail the fiduciary nature of the relationship between the Crown and Aboriginal peoples. In the *Sparrow* case, for example, the court stated that "the Government has the responsibility to act in a fiduciary capacity with respect to aboriginal peoples. The relationship between the Government and aboriginals is trustlike."[33] My point is simply to indicate that the law of trusts has very little to offer if our hope is to understand the fiduciary relationship between Aboriginal peoples and the Crown.

Interestingly, the court characterized the relationship between Aboriginal peoples and the Crown as "fiduciary" in nature prior to 1982 in a number of cases unrelated to section 35.[34] And yet, the precise nature and scope of this relationship – including important details such as the Crown's fiduciary duties toward Aboriginal Canadians – remained for the most part unclear until the early part of the twenty-first century. Beginning in 2004, a series of section 35 cases – most importantly, *Haida Nation, Mikisew Cree, Rio Tinto, Taku River,* and *Tsilhqot'in* – came before the SCC, and the rulings in these cases provided much-needed clarity on these issues.[35]

According to the SCC, when government action infringes an Aboriginal right (both a recognized right and a potentially existing right), the Crown has an obligation to consult, and under certain circumstances accommodate, the Aboriginal holders of this right (Hogg 2009, 12–15). The court has established that the degree of consultation and accommodation required varies on a case-by-case basis, ranging from mere notification of government action to requiring Aboriginal consent for government action. Exactly what is required in any given case depends on the nature of the government infringement and the severity of its consequences on the Aboriginal right in question.[36] In the case of a right that is not yet established, the strength of the Aboriginal group's claim is also a factor.[37] In any case, if the Crown acts to pursue a legitimate legislative objective and discharges its fiduciary duties when it infringes an Aboriginal right (by consulting and/or accommodating Aboriginal peoples), the infringement is justified and, thus, is lawful.

While the analysis thus far has centred primarily on activity-based Aboriginal rights, Aboriginal peoples may also make territorial claims (i.e., claims to title over traditional lands). In the 1997 *Delgamuukw* case, the SCC spelled out the basic nature and scope of Aboriginal title. And in 2014, the court handed down the *Tsilhqot'in* decision, which included the first and only instance of a judicial declaration of Aboriginal title in Canada. The *Tsilhqot'in* case has resulted in a great deal of excitement – indeed, phrases such as "game changer" and "new direction" have been used in media. Some have even speculated, with great optimism, that the decision may represent the beginning of a new era in Aboriginal-state relations in Canada.

In a report on the *Tsilhqot'in* decision for the MacDonald-Laurier Institute, Kenneth Coates and Dwight Newman (2014, 1) encourage us not to be blinded by all of the media hype surrounding the decision. In my view, Coates and Newman are right to call for tempered optimism. After all, it is too soon to predict how *Tsilhqot'in* will impact Aboriginal rights over the long term, let alone how the decision will impact the relationship between Aboriginal peoples and the state. The *Tsilhqot'in* decision is important because it provided a number of clarifications and addressed some serious questions about Aboriginal title that have cropped up since *Delgamuukw*.[38] Given that little time has elapsed since the *Tsilhqot'in* decision, academic work on it is a bit scanty, but scholars such as Senwung Luk (2014) and Jonnette Watson Hamilton (2014) seem to hold a view of the decision that is similar to mine.

In its 1997 *Delgamuukw* decision, the SCC stated that Aboriginal title "is a distinct species of aboriginal right that was recognized and affirmed by s. 35(1)."[39] In effect, Aboriginal title is a subset of the Aboriginal rights covered by section 35, and so the legal tests outlined thus far inform the process for establishing and securing this form of title. However, the tests for Aboriginal title do differ in some important respects from the tests described above. In *Delgamuukw*, Chief Justice Lamer explained that Aboriginal title is summarized by two propositions: "First, that aboriginal title encompasses the right to exclusive use and occupation of the land held pursuant to that title for a variety of purposes ... and second, that those protected uses must not be irreconcilable with the nature of the group's attachment to that land."[40]

The first proposition outlined the justices' view that Aboriginal title is a right to specific territories, where "the title-holding group has the right to choose the uses to which the land is put and to enjoy its economic fruits."[41] But what, exactly, grounds such a right? Or what does the court think is the basis for holding Aboriginal title? In the *Tshilhqot'in* case, the court stated that "Aboriginal title to land is based on 'occupation' prior to the assertion of European sovereignty."[42] It went on to clarify that only occupation of a certain type would suffice to ground Aboriginal title; namely, occupation has to be "sufficient," "continuous," and "exclusive."[43]

The "sufficiency" condition can be satisfied by actual occupation (e.g., the existence of settled Aboriginal communities) or by the way in which the land was used by the Aboriginal claimants where settled communities do not exist. As the court explained in the *Tsilhqot'in* case, "Aboriginal title is not confined to specific sites of settlement but extends to tracts of land that were regularly used for hunting, fishing or otherwise exploiting resources and over which the group exercised effective control at the time of assertion of European sovereignty."[44] The temporal condition – that occupation be "continuous" – relates to the reliance on present occupation as the basis for an Aboriginal title claim. It is important to illustrate a link between the group's current occupancy of a particular territory and occupancy of this same territory before the Crown asserted sovereignty. The court insisted in the *Tsilhqot'in* ruling that "continuity simply means that for evidence of present occupation to establish an inference of pre-sovereignty occupation, the present occupation must be rooted in pre-sovereignty times."[45] In terms of the exclusivity condition, the court was clear that the term "exclusive" should be interpreted to mean "intention and capacity to control land."[46] This way of understanding "exclusive" includes a range of modes of occupation, from actual exclusive control of land (such that all other potential users' access is regulated by the group claiming title) to a group's demonstrating an effort or intention to control the claimed land.[47] Finally, the onus of illustrating that Aboriginal title exists falls on the Aboriginal claimants.[48] The SCC sums up the matter thus: "In asking whether Aboriginal title is established, the general requirements are: (1) 'sufficient occupation' of the land claimed to establish title at the time of assertion of European sovereignty; (2) continuity of occupation where present occupation is relied on; and (3) exclusive historic occupation."[49]

The second proposition outlined by Chief Justice Lamer – that "protected uses must not be irreconcilable with the nature of the group's attachment to that land"[50] – basically means that Aboriginal title has a built-in limit. Aboriginal title lands cannot be used for any purpose that would undermine the Aboriginal group's original claim to that land. For example, an Aboriginal group could not strip-mine its territory, because doing so would (probably) render occupancy, or the land uses cited to demonstrate occupancy, impossible.

Similar in kind to other section 35 rights, Aboriginal title is not absolute. The Crown can infringe on this right by following the same procedure outlined for justifying the infringement of activity-based Aboriginal rights.[51] The second part of the justification process that deals with the question of the honour of the Crown, however, differs when the right at issue is Aboriginal title. For example, the fiduciary relationship between Aboriginal peoples and the Crown requires that Aboriginal peoples be consulted about the ways in which their lands will be used. According to the court, engaging in such consultations may be enough to satisfy the honour of the Crown.[52] Moreover, when Aboriginal title is infringed, fair compensation must be provided to the holders of that title.[53]

In the process of spelling out the legal tests for Aboriginal title, the SCC has included some interesting comments regarding the character of this property right. First, Aboriginal title is always held by a collective (e.g., an Aboriginal community or nation), as opposed to other land titles in Canada that may be held by individuals.[54] Second, whereas other types of title are the result of grants made after the British Crown asserted sovereignty, the source of Aboriginal title is the occupancy of land and its use by Aboriginal peoples before the assertion of Crown sovereignty.[55] Finally, unlike other forms of title, Aboriginal title is inalienable – in the sense that it can only be surrendered to the Crown.[56] Together, the legal test for Aboriginal title and its particular characteristics render it like no other kind of property right in Canada. Aboriginal title is unique – to use the court's words, it is "a sui generis interest in land."[57]

This overview of the legal tests for activity-based and territorial claims highlights a number of factors for those interested in the nature and scope of the rights covered by section 35. First, it exposes that Aboriginal rights can only be based on particular types of claims. These claims are limited in nature in that they must be rooted in Aboriginal practices, customs, and traditions or occupancy. They are also limited in scope, for they must find their source in the pre-contact or pre-control periods. Moreover, they must have survived at least until the patriation of the Constitution (meaning that no surrender or extinguishment of the right occurred before 1982). Second, this overview of the legal tests highlights the substantial burdens placed on Aboriginal claimants and the Crown in a dispute involving Aboriginal rights. The former must demonstrate the existence of a right and its prima facie infringement, while the latter must prove justifiable infringement.

An examination of the jurisprudential framework supports the argument that section 35 aims to accommodate Aboriginal peoples by protecting their collective identities. For one thing, the jurisprudential framework defines section 35 rights as rights to engage in pre-contact or pre-control practices, customs, and traditions, and the activities must be integral to Aboriginal cultures. The logic here is that ensuring that Aboriginal peoples are able to continue to engage in these activities is a way of maintaining Aboriginal cultures. Along the same lines, the jurisprudential framework defines Aboriginal title as the right to land that was exclusively occupied (or used in certain ways) by Aboriginal groups before the assertion of Crown sovereignty. Again, the right of groups to hold lands that were held by past members (and, therefore, the right to live where past members lived and use the land as past members used it) is a mechanism for the maintenance of Aboriginal cultures. In effect, the tests developed by the SCC protect aboriginality by extending protection to Aboriginal cultures.

Indeed, a significant amount of academic commentary on Canadian Aboriginal rights jurisprudence highlights the important role occupied by Aboriginal cultures and aboriginality in section 35 jurisprudence. For example, in their analysis of the *Van der Peet* decision, scholars Russel Lawrence Barsh and James Youngblood Henderson (1997, 997) explain how, for the SCC justices, it is "the courts' task to ascertain 'the crucial elements of those pre-existing distinctive societies,' which is to say those elements that are 'integral' to the identity of each First Nation." Referring to the *Sparrow* case, legal scholar Patrick Macklem (1997a, 108) argues that "in the Court's opinion, the practice [of fishing] deserves the status of a constitutional right because it was and is integral to Aboriginal culture and identity." Similarly, in commenting on the *Van der Peet* case, legal scholar Gordon Christie (2003, 483) advances that the "Supreme Court has determined that Aboriginal rights are meant to protect 'Aboriginality,' which is understood to encompass those aspects of traditional Aboriginal cultures that define these cultures as peculiarly 'Aboriginal' in nature." These comments on section 35 jurisprudence highlight that aboriginality is the cornerstone of the SCC's construction of Aboriginal rights and that the purpose of these rights is to safeguard the Aboriginal collective identity.[58]

Conclusion

The review of the jurisprudence on Aboriginal rights in Canada and its corresponding academic commentary presented in this chapter reveals that the SCC departed significantly from the positions advocated by the Aboriginal participants and the Crown during the four constitutional meetings of the 1980s. Contrary to the insistence of the government representatives, Aboriginal rights would not be a primarily symbolic political gesture, nor would they be, as the Aboriginal participants hoped, a declaration of Aboriginal self-determination. Instead, the SCC decided that Aboriginal rights would be about aboriginality. More specifically, Aboriginal rights would be about the protection of Aboriginal peoples' collective identities.

By tying section 35 to aboriginality, the court set up a situation in which disputes involving the constitutional provision would turn on the question of what precisely is required to protect the collective identity. As a result, section 35 litigation would take the following form: Is the right to X required in situation Y in order to protect the collective identity of Aboriginal nation Z? Notice how this structure presupposes one important thing: that all of the parties agree on the meaning of Aboriginal nation Z's identity. However, as will become evident over the course of the next few chapters, aboriginality is a contested phenomenon. The contested nature of the collective identity puts into question the plausibility of holding this a priori assumption about aboriginality and, as a result, the wisdom of shackling Aboriginal rights to that collective identity.

2

Competing Approaches
and Conceptualizations of Aboriginality

Who are the Aboriginal peoples of Canada? Aboriginal peoples have been variously described as Canadians citizens, full stop (Flanagan 2000); as citizens who have a bundle of special rights that go above and beyond those accorded to citizens generally (Cairns 2000); as individuals who can make certain egalitarian claims against the state because they have been (and still are) subjected to systemic discrimination (Jung 2008); as members of distinctive nations that are entitled to jurisdictional authority over specific peoples and territories (Ladner 2005); and as members of nations that can make freedom-based claims against modern settler states because these states continue the colonial relationship established by their imperial predecessors (Tully 2000a). While this list is not by any means exhaustive, it is meant to illustrate a (small) degree of the variety of meanings shouldered by the term "Aboriginal."

What explains the lack of agreement over the meaning of this collective identity? In the examples above, the conceptions of aboriginality differ on multiple levels. First, the constitutive elements that make up each definition of the collective identity vary. Aboriginal peoples are: Canadians, Canadians with extra rights, subjects of discrimination, members of distinctive nations, and subjects of colonial domination. Second, some of the constitutive elements that make up each definition not only vary, but represent different kinds of difference. The first two definitions of aboriginality above are based on traits – specifically, the notion that a person must possess (or fails to possess) a certain set of traits in order to be part of a group. That is, Aboriginal peoples either possess the same traits as every other Canadian

(Flanagan's definition) or possess extra rights (Cairns's definition). Contrastingly, the last three definitions are based on the existence of a set of specific relations – relations of inequality (for Jung, the relations are about interpersonal inequality; for Ladner, inter-group inequality) and relations of domination (for Tully, colonial domination). Thus, if we focus on just these three ways of understanding aboriginality, we get the following definitions: Aboriginal peoples are Canadians who are treated unequally by non-Aboriginal Canadians (Jung's definition), are members of distinctive political communities that are denied the same treatment enjoyed by the Canadian political community (Ladner's definition), or are members of currently dominated political communities (Tully's definition).

The lack of agreement over the meaning of Aboriginal collective identity in the five examples above is a result of both a divergence of opinion regarding what it takes to be Aboriginal (the question of which traits and relations should be included), as well as a divergence of opinion regarding how to approach the conceptualization of the collective identity (the question of whether traits, relations, or both should be the basis of this identity). In my view, before analyzing the way in which the parties to section 35 cases characterize aboriginality and the consequences of these characterizations, valuable insights can be gained from familiarity with the extent and character of the contestation surrounding the collective identity. In this chapter, I highlight some of the differences between various conceptualizations of aboriginality outlined in the scholarly literature. My intention is not to provide a comprehensive typology or analysis of all conceptualizations of aboriginality in the literature.[1] Following the lead of scholars such as Bruce Granville Miller (2003), my specific focus is on how conceptions based on traits and inter-group relations lead to fundamentally different definitions of aboriginality. This focus is important because in the court material, the participants cite both traits and relations when they characterize aboriginality. As a result, it becomes necessary to determine which approach is best for an analysis of section 35.

Traits-Based Approaches
Perhaps the most common way of defining aboriginality (or any collective identity, for that matter) is to cite a list of traits that members of the group are believed to share. Not surprisingly then, many scholarly

conceptualizations of aboriginality rely on the presence of particular traits in order to construct a version of this collective identity. Typically, these conceptualizations work by, first, identifying significant elements that are presented as constitutive of an aboriginal identity; second, justifying the significance of these traits (i.e., providing reasons for why these traits – and not others – are of definitional significance); and third, using these traits as a litmus test for aboriginality. Traits such as descent, attachment to land, shared practices, common values, associative duties, and particular relations to time and space have all formed the basis of different versions of Aboriginal identity.

For some, the question of who is Aboriginal can be settled by tracing an individual's lineage and establishing a biological or kinship link to a particular group or people. Approaching aboriginality in this fashion produces the following type of definition: "[Aboriginal] people are thought to be recognizable by descent from significant historical people (such as treaty signers) or genealogically from known indigenous people of an earlier period. They are thought, then, to be recognizable as those who received promises from the state ... and their descendants" (Miller 2003, 52). In this instance, the significant constitutive element of aboriginality is the notion of a particular descent or genealogy. We can see this type of conception in action in the use of blood quantum requirements in the United States and band lists in Canada to establish who is and who is not (legally) Aboriginal. The work of Indigenous studies scholar Bonita Lawrence (2004) illustrates the serious and oftentimes negative consequences for Aboriginal individuals and communities of government policies based on such determinants of aboriginality, one of the most important being the gradually smaller and smaller number of people capable of meeting such requirements.

Connection to a particular territory or homeland is another marker commonly cited in trait-based approaches to aboriginality. In her work on national identity, political philosopher Margaret Moore (2001, 176) advances that theories of nationalism often include territorial considerations (such as a group's sense of entitlement to a specific homeland) because attachments to particular places are at times important to a people's sense of who they are. What Moore highlights is that certain groups' collective identities have an important territorial component; that is, they can only be adequately defined by reference to their sense of connection to particular territories. Indeed, a number of scholars conceptualize aboriginality in just such a fashion. Historian Arthur J. Ray (1996, 1), for example, proposes that "many of Canada's Indigenous peoples define themselves in terms of the homelands that sustained their ancestors." For his part, legal scholar Gordon Christie (2004, 241) explains that, "for many Aboriginal people, lands and resources are thought of as inextricably connected to the people; indeed, this connection can be so strong, and of such a nature, that it goes into forming collective and individual identities."

Under the traits-based approach, a collection of shared cultural, spiritual, and political practices can also form the basis of an Aboriginal identity. The potlatch, the sun dance, the feast, the raising of a totem, and many other practices are cited as constitutive elements of aboriginality. In other words, the question of who is Aboriginal would be answered by citing a collection of shared practices. However, practices are not the only way to base a conception of aboriginality on spiritual, cultural, or political considerations.

A particularly fascinating example of such an approach is advanced by Indigenous politics scholar Taiaiake Alfred. Alfred (1999, xvi) argues that aboriginality is centred on the notion of a commitment to a particular normative vision that includes cultural, spiritual, and political considerations. Specifically, a key feature of this identity is a commitment to a particular political tradition that is characterized by the values of respect, balance, and harmony. While he acknowledges the existence of a vast diversity of practices within the community of North American Aboriginal nations, Alfred (1999, xvi) accounts for this pluralism by explaining that "there may be 500 different ways of expressing these values, but in our singular commitment to them we find what is perhaps the only pan-Indian commonality." He goes on to explain that this political tradition differs from other (i.e., non-Aboriginal) political traditions not because of the inclusion of these values (for other political traditions may advocate similar values), but in "the prioritization of those values, the rigorous consistency of its principles with those values, and the pattern and procedures of government" (Alfred 1999, 24).

Along similar lines, associative duties can form the basis of a characterization of aboriginality. Generally, an associative duty is defined as a duty that arises as a result of membership in a particular group and that places individuals under certain special obligations. These obligations are "special" because they are not universally held and can, at times, override individuals' general obligations (Scheffler 2001, 48). For philosophers, the most important of these general obligations are (probably) our natural duties, which are nonvoluntary obligations that we hold as a result of being members of the human species. Natural duties are owed to all of humanity, as opposed to a specific person or group. Commonly cited examples include the duty of charity and the duty to render assistance (when doing so will not put one in harm's way). Contrastingly, examples of associative duties include duties owed by parents to their children (and vice versa). The concept of an associative duty helps us to understand why it is morally acceptable, in certain circumstances, for parents to favour their own children at the expense of other people's children or for children to favour their own parents. And so, in the horrifying scenario where a person comes across a group of drowning children and one of the children belongs to the individual in question, we would not find that person morally blameworthy if he attempted to rescue his child before attempting to rescue any other. We would, however, find this same person's behaviour blameworthy if he saved all of the Caucasian children first. In this instance, we accept one form of favouritism (i.e., saving one's own child) while rejecting another (i.e., saving a child based on race) because we acknowledge that people have special obligations that can impact how they should behave.

Associative duties can be important in the characterization of a collective identity. That is, one can establish a definition of a collective identity by identifying a list of associative duties that are considered important by a particular group. In terms of aboriginality, a number of scholars advance that the collective identity entails a particular set of associative duties related to such things as the land or the natural world; they generally characterize Aboriginal peoples as stewards of certain territories. Legal scholar Darlene Johnston (1989, 32), for example, states that Aboriginal people "view their relationship with the land as central to their collective identity and well-being," and she advances that "Native people regard themselves as trustees of the land for future generations." Johnston cites an associative duty related to the land and the unborn as the basis for her articulation of this collective identity. Scholars of Indigenous politics Ovide Mercredi and Mary Ellen

Turpel (1993, 33) include a similar notion of a special obligation in their characterization of aboriginality; they explain that "our identities and rights as distinct peoples flow from our relationship to the land." They go on to characterize this relationship to the land as an associative duty of care which Aboriginal peoples share:

> We have always been here on this land we call Turtle Island [North America], on our homelands given to us by the Creator, and we have a responsibility to care for and live in harmony with all of her creations. We believe that the responsibility to care for this land was given to us by our Creator, the Great Spirit. It is a sacred obligation, which means the First peoples must care for all of Creation in fulfilling this responsibility. (Mercredi and Turpel 1993, 16)

Like Johnston, Mercredi and Turpel put forward a conception of aboriginality that includes a set of associative duties that is unique to the people who bear the collective identity and that is advanced as a constitutive element of the collective identity. In this instance, "Who are we?" is answered by reference to the set of associative duties "we" hold in common.

The traits-based approach also includes constitutive elements that go beyond associative duties; descent; connections to land or nature; shared cultural, spiritual, and political practices; and values. Conceptions of aboriginality under this approach may be based on less concrete considerations. For example, the collective identity can be, and indeed has been, defined vis-à-vis a group's relations to time and space. This explains why some scholars argue that aboriginality is characterized by "time depth, antiquity, and primordialism" (Miller 2003, 53). The historical reach of the group is what defines its identity. Thus, a group is Aboriginal because it can trace its origins back through millennia.

A traits-based approach can also work in reverse. In other words, aboriginality may be primarily characterized by the absence of particular traits. From this view, some argue that members of certain groups are Aboriginal because their ancestors were not Christian; because their societies were not part of the Western Enlightenment tradition; or because they are not members of ethnic groups, minorities, or the peasantry (Miller 2003, 52–53). Political scientist Tom Flanagan presents just such a portrait of Aboriginal peoples. His conception of aboriginality is constructed around what he believes the collective identity does not entail. Flanagan (2000, 37) argues that Aboriginal peoples were not civilized,[2] lack sovereignty, and, as collectives, do not meet the criteria of nationhood. He puts forward that an absence of intensive agricultural practices, urbanization, division of labour, adequate intellectual achievements (such as record keeping and writing), technological sophistication, and a state system demonstrate that Aboriginal societies did not reach the level of advancement required in order to be classified as civilized (Flanagan 2000, 33). Flanagan (2000, 59) contends that "sovereignty in the strict sense exists only in the organized states characteristic of civilized societies." According to his logic, since Aboriginal societies were uncivilized, sovereignty could not inhere in them. Lastly, in terms of nationhood, Flanagan (2000, 84–86) advances that the standard notion of the term "nation" includes criteria such as an adequate level of civilization, significance (meaning the existence of a substantial population and landmass), control over territory, solidarity, and sovereignty. He argues that Aboriginal societies do not satisfy these criteria for nationhood and concludes that "the objective attributes of Indian bands are far from what nations are generally understood to be" (Flanagan 2000, 97). In sum, Flanagan's conception of the collective identity hinges on what Aboriginal people lack: To be Aboriginal means to lack a certain degree of civilization, sovereignty, and nationhood.

Anthropologist Richard J. Perry also focuses on an absence of certain traits when conceptualizing aboriginality. In contrast to Flanagan, however, he advances that this collective identity is coterminous with the absence of a state. Specifically, Perry (1996, 8) puts forward the argument that "the term 'indigenous peoples' refers ... to local populations that existed in place before a state system incorporated them." For Perry, it is the absence of a modern state – as opposed to a lack of civilization, sovereignty, or nationhood – that plays a decisive role. Perry's definition of Aboriginal peoples underpins his characterization of the purpose of his research. He states that his work explores "what happens when people whose ancestors have lived for centuries in small, autonomous societies find themselves encompassed within state systems" (Perry 1996, xi). Perry resolves the issue of how to define aboriginality by illustrating the consequences of being involuntarily incorporated into a state system.

In most cases, a number of traits are cited in combination as the basis for a conceptualization of aboriginality. That is, scholars usually do not define aboriginality by relying on a single trait. For example, anthropologist Ronald Niezen (2003b, xvi) takes the position that the collective identity "is based on notions of family and community, ancestral wisdom, permanent homelands, and cultural durability." This underpins his contention that aboriginality "refers to a primordial identity, to people with primary attachments to land and culture, 'traditional' people with lasting connections to ways of life that have survived 'from time immemorial'" (Niezen 2003b, 3). A number of traits – including descent, connection to land, shared practices and values, and particular relations to time and space – come together to form Niezen's version of aboriginality. Taiaiake Alfred and Jeff Corntassel (2005, 608) also employ a number of these traits to construct their definition of the collective identity; they advance that Aboriginal peoples "have long understood their existence as peoples or nations ... as framed around axes of land, culture and community." They go on to explain that "building on this notion of a dynamic and interconnected concept of Indigenous identity constituted in history, ceremony, language and land, we consider relationships (or kinship networks) to be at the core of an authentic Indigenous identity" (Alfred and Corntassel 2005, 609). For scholars who employ a traits-based approach, the meaning of aboriginality comes down to the traits the members of this group are said to share. As a result, the academic debate can often turn on the question of which traits best characterize aboriginality.

Relational Approaches

A number of scholars reject the idea that a set of traits can produce an adequate conceptualization of collective identity. For many of these scholars, the proper way to proceed is to build a conception of identity around a set of relations. Two types of relations, inter-group and intra-group, are relevant for our purposes. By inter-group relations, I mean the existing (mostly objective) differences between groups (e.g., group-based differences in resources, opportunities, power). Together, these differences constitute a group's social location or situated position. By intra-group relations, I mean the affective features that mark group-based membership (e.g., the bonds of attachment that group members feel for one another) and how group members treat one another.

Relational approaches to collective identity differ when it comes to the role allocated to inter-group and intra-group relations; some conceptualizations stress the former, while others stress the latter. In my view, both inter-group and intra-group relations are important and this is reflected in the analysis of relational approaches outlined in this chapter and the next.

Social anthropologist Thomas Hylland Eriksen is an important and prominent advocate of the relational approach to collective identity. Eriksen (1993, 9–10) argues that "group identities must always be defined in relation to that which they are not – in other words, in relation to non-members of the group." Examining Eriksen's understanding of aboriginality can shed some light on how relational approaches to this collective identity work.

There are two central elements to Eriksen's relational approach to collective identity. First, aboriginality is not defined by a catalogue of identifiable traits. The substantive contents of the collective identity are markers of a particular situated position occupied by a group in relation to another group. Stated differently, the substantive contents are the relations that exist between at least two groups. Accordingly, Eriksen (1992, 5) advances that Aboriginal peoples are "politically non-dominant" and that their culture is not the one "championed by the state." In Eriksen's definition, the important element is the subordinate position (politically and culturally) of one group in relation to another (i.e., the group's situated position).

Second, even when Eriksen refers to traits by indicating that Aboriginal peoples share a list of features, these features work to emphasize a relational position. His list includes, "(i) territorial claims not respected by governments; (ii) threats of 'cultural genocide,' that is, enforced assimilation or physical extermination; (iii) a way of life requiring special measures in economic, political and/or educational matters" (Eriksen 1992, 6). This list reveals that the position of Aboriginal peoples (in terms of access to and title over land, cultural difference and security, and rights) relative to non-Aboriginals is the primary consideration. Eriksen's conceptualization of aboriginality speaks of a particular situated position rather than a package of characteristics that a group of individuals shares. That is, collective identity turns on inter-group relations.

Political scientist Tim Schouls also advances a relational conception of aboriginality that highlights the significance of inter-group relations. More specifically, Schouls (2003, 51) argues that "all Aboriginal peoples are products of the interrelationships between Euro-Canadian settlers and the original occupants of the land." He adds that aboriginality "carries with it the idea that the group of people to whom the term applies were subordinated by the settler state, treated as outsiders, and regarded as inferiors" (Schouls 2003, 51).

According to Schouls (2003, 53–54), cultural and national elements are important elements of aboriginality not because aboriginality inheres in them, but because they serve as points of identification for the group, allowing the members of the group to police the boundaries of group belonging. For Schouls, these elements are instrumental. Aboriginality does not inherently rely on any particular cultural or national element (or set of elements):

> Conspicuously absent in this formulation of identity is any formal requirement that identification by individuals with their Aboriginal communities must be based on shared attributes of culture or nationhood. Of course, Aboriginal individuals may share one or more attributes of culture or nationhood, and these attributes may well serve to differentiate them from non-Aboriginal people. But the point is that the character of the relationship and the strength of the boundaries between aboriginal communities and the Canadian state need not by definition be connected to the resiliency of cultural and national differences. (Schouls 2003, 52)

Schouls' work is illustrative because it touches on the affective aspect of collective identity. In the passage above, Schouls explains how intergroup relations can create the right circumstances for the development of bonds of attachment between group members. More precisely, Schouls outlines one of the links between inter-group and intra-group relations by arguing that people can form ties with one another as a result of being subjected to the same inter-group dynamics. Bonds of attachment felt by members of a particular group can develop because many of the members of the group interact in a very particular way with most of the members of another group.

Moreover, Schouls's work demonstrates how elements such as cultural traits and national characteristics – elements which, upon first glance, would seem to be most appropriate for traits-based approaches to conceptualizations of aboriginality – may be important components of conceptualizations that result from relational approaches. Schouls reveals that the role that these elements play in relational approaches, however, is different than the role they play in traits-based approaches. In traits-based approaches, they constitute the meaning of the collective identity; that is, they are items on the "checklist" of the identity. In contrast, in relational approaches, those elements are employed in order to clarify the situated position of one group in relation to another by doing such things as outlining the boundary between group insiders and outsiders. For example, the fact that one group's mother tongue is Cree and another's is English is not important in and of itself. Language becomes important only when social, economic, or political inequalities correspond to this cleavage – that is, when Cree speakers are disadvantaged in significant ways in relation to their English-speaking counterparts. And experiencing the ill effects of inequality can form the basis for a shared experience that generates bonds of solidarity between members of the subordinate group. From this view, cultural and national attributes are important only insofar as they help us to trace the inter-group and intra-group relations.

From the relational point of view, characteristics such as language are not the essential building blocks of a definition of the Aboriginal collective identity; inter-group and intra-group relations perform that function. In this way, scholars who employ relational approaches can (and indeed do) include cultural traits and national characteristics in their conceptualizations of aboriginality, but they do so with very different purposes than their counterparts who favour traits-based approaches.

Conclusion

This overview of the ways in which scholars employ traits-based and relational approaches when conceptualizing aboriginality is intended to demonstrate that when scholars refer to aboriginality, there is far from any guarantee that they are advancing the same understanding of the collective identity. It is more likely, in fact, that they have very different things in mind. This survey of the different conceptions of aboriginality highlights the fact that before one can assess the impact of aboriginality on the controversy surrounding Aboriginal rights in Canada – let alone what to do about it – other decisions need to be made, including working out which approach should be used to conceptualize the collective identity in the first place. The next chapter presents a comparative analysis of the two approaches and advances that one approach – the relational approach – is, in fact, the better choice.

3

The Case for a Relational Approach

Aboriginality can and does have a plethora of possible meanings. And a significant degree of this definitional multiplicity results from the competing approaches used to conceptualize the collective identity. This raises the question of which approach is most appropriate if one aims to conduct an investigation of aboriginality and the Canadian jurisprudence on Aboriginal rights. The traits-based approach and the relational approach – like all conceptual tools – manifest certain shortcomings when they are employed to explain political phenomena. Determining which approach is best for the task at hand depends on an assessment of these drawbacks.

There are, of course, many ways to go about building a comparison. I am interested in assessing the analytical and the real-world costs associated with each way of conceptualizing aboriginality. By analytical costs, I mean what scholars generally have in mind when they assess a concept or theory, such as the explanatory power of the concept or theory (e.g., how well the concept or theory explains the phenomenon of interest), as well as its rigour (e.g., its internal coherence and logic, its parsimoniousness and elegance, its consistency with concepts and theories that treat related phenomena, and the like).

I use the phrase "real-world costs" to refer to the costs shouldered by people as a result of the decision to employ certain theories and concepts (instead of the possible alternatives) in our attempts to understand our everyday world. I am primarily interested in the link between theory and practice highlighted by many scholars, especially those with a primarily critical orientation. For example, feminist scholars such as Carole Pateman (1988) have illustrated how the concept of contract has negatively impacted the lives of women in numerous ways by facilitating their economic exploitation and political subordination.[1] Along the same lines, some postmodernists, such as Judith Butler (2001), have revealed how the concept of biological sex negatively impacts human beings (especially intersexed persons) by providing a ready justification for "medical" intervention against minds and bodies that do not conform with existing biological sex norms. This list of examples could be quite extensive. My main point is that our theories and concepts matter not just because they can impact our degree of understanding of real-world phenomena, but also because they can have a real impact on people's lives (e.g., how people see themselves, how people see one another, and most importantly, how people treat one another).

I concede that it is not always easy to determine whether a concept or theory produces only (or even mostly) analytical costs or real-world costs. There is a significant empirical component to making such a determination, which raises many practical problems. For example, in order to say that a concept or theory has a real-world cost, one has to establish a causal link between a concept or theory and an instance of harm – and this can be quite challenging. This task is further complicated by the fact that concepts can come in "bundled" form, making it difficult to trace the causal mechanisms at work. For example, theories usually include numerous concepts, and it can be difficult to establish a causal link between one particular concept and an instance of harm. I believe that these problems can be overcome by careful social science and so I assume that it is possible to make the distinction between analytical and real-world costs. I also assume that other difficulties of an empirical nature not identified here can be similarly addressed.

Putting aside these empirical matters, I want to focus on the important normative facets of the distinction between analytical and real-world costs. Specifically, I am interested in the relative moral weight of each of these costs. My basic claim is that the costs that are shouldered by people (i.e., real-world costs) should be considered of primary import and thus, are more worthy of our concern. Contrastingly, costs that do not impact people in direct ways (e.g., analytical costs), while still of interest and significance, should be considered less weighty and so merit less of our concern. I think, at times, scholars (and certain types of philosophers are particularly prone to this) fixate on analytical costs, paying insufficient attention to the ways in which concepts and theories make people worse off. I advance that a concept or theory that has real-world costs is inferior to one that manifests only analytical costs. I argue that relational approaches produce significant analytical costs, but they are better than traits-based approaches because traits-based approaches produce real-world costs.

Analytical Costs of Relational Approaches

Relational approaches generate two analytical costs when employed to construct a conception of aboriginality. The first cost is that they often present collective identity as a primarily instrumental phenomenon, while in everyday life, we generally characterize identity in a noninstrumental fashion. The second analytical cost is that relational approaches tend to overemphasize the role played by nongroup members in defining collective identity – that is, they generally focus on what group outsiders have to say about the identity, rather than on what group insiders have to say about it.

What does it mean to say that collective identity is characterized as a purely instrumental phenomenon? What I have in mind are scholarly accounts of collective identities that describe them as the means for particular groups to secure certain interests. (Given the nature of the work pursued herein, political interests are of particular interest.) From this view, collective identity is valuable to individuals because it facilitates the achievement of those interests and is defined primarily by reference to that function. The work of political scientist Courtney Jung on aboriginality illustrates the point. According to Jung (2003, 4), Aboriginal identity is the product of twenty-first-century politics and is best understood in light of the political project pursued by the groups called "Aboriginal." She contends that the Aboriginal collective identity is actually a label for class politics that arises as a result of the neo-liberal reordering of relations between the state and other important stakeholders (Jung 2003, 4–5). These basic propositions lead Jung (2003, 30) to conclude that the world's rural poor have employed indigenous identity in order to carve out a space for political activism at the domestic level, and have been able, by invoking their identity as indigenous people, to enter a global political dialogue ... Although indigenous identity locates them in a distinct political space, from which they can establish new alliances and make different demands, indigenous identity plays a role that is functionally similar, in established political voice, to peasant identity in a prior era.

What is significant in Jung's statement is the fact that aboriginality (i.e., its meaning) is reduced to the strategic deployment of a collective identity to pursue a particular set of interests that were previously pursued by a class-based identity (i.e., the rural poor or peasantry). In this case, the collective identity is important because of its political use-value and it is defined primarily in terms of this value. Jung presents a sort of functionalist definition of aboriginality.

Now, I do not believe (nor am I arguing) that identity cannot be in-strumentally valuable. People certainly use their collective identity for strategic purposes. For example, when one claims to have special knowledge about a certain topic (e.g., homophobia) because one belongs to a particular identity group (e.g., the person identifies as a member of the LGBTQ community), that person is, in effect, deploying identity instrumentally in order to justify a claim of epistemic privilege. And on its face, there is nothing wrong or nefarious about this type of behaviour.[2]

I argue that it is a mistake to reduce the meaning of collective identities (especially of the ethnocultural and national varieties) to their (possible) strategic uses. Collective identities are also important to people for non-instrumental reasons – I think many of us would agree with this point. After all, history is full of examples of people holding on (very tightly) to their collective identities in the face of overwhelming societal pressure to adopt some other collective identity. If collective identities were simply strategic resources, people would be quite willing to change them whenever doing so would be politically, economically, or socially advantageous. Moreover, this instrumentalist characterization seems inconsistent with how people often describe their own collective identities. People often talk about their identities in the context of trying to explain who they are, as opposed to the political or economic interests they may have. Thus, a purely (or even primarily) instrumental understanding of the concept fails to capture what people mean when they refer to collective identity or why it is important to them.

The second analytical cost of relational approaches to conceptualizing collective identity is that they tend to place a great deal of stock in the role played by nonmembers in identity definition, and some view this role as overly determinative. For example, in the case of Aboriginal peoples, Alfred and Corntassel (2005, 606) argue that this type of approach "emphasizes interaction with non-indigenous people in precipitating identity awareness and personal change, and de-emphasizes relationships with communities and families." They conclude that, as a consequence, only a minimal number of scholarly conceptualizations of aboriginality reflect Aboriginal perspectives of the collective identity (Alfred and Corntassel 2005, 605). They suggest that reserving too great a role for nonmembers (and relations with nonmembers) in the process of identity formation and maintenance decreases the participation of the actual bearers of the collective identity in the process of group definition. And if intra-group relations are to play a role in an understanding of any given collective identity, then some members of the group need to be consulted. How else can we trace the affective dimensions of a particular collective identity?

In short, Alfred and Corntassel are probably right, and we should be cautious about these conceptualizations of aboriginality. At the very least, we should endeavour to discover what was "crowded out" of the versions of aboriginality created by non-Aboriginals.

Real-World Costs of Traits-Based Approaches

Traits-based approaches have their own set of costs. They produce real-world costs, as well as analytical costs – as opposed to relational approaches, which produce only analytical costs. Given my claim about the moral priority of real-world costs – that is, that they have more moral weight than their analytical counterparts – I focus only on the real-world costs. After all, if one approach manifests only analytical costs, then one only need establish that the other approach manifests at least some real-world costs in order to argue that the latter is inferior, at least on this one dimension of comparison.

Many of the real-world costs produced by traits-based approaches stem from the fact that the approaches present collective identity as settled or fixed. This leaves them open to the charge of essentialism. There is an impressive array of scholarship focused on essentialism and its effects on group members and conceptualizations of collective identity. What do scholars mean when they say that a conception of identity is "essentialist"? English professor Diana Fuss (1989, xi) puts forward that "essence is most commonly understood as a belief in the real, true essence of things, the invariable and fixed properties which define the 'whatness' of a given entity." Accordingly, an essentialist conception of identity is premised on the idea that it is possible to identify the "whatness" or properties that make up a given identity and that this "whatness" is, for the most part, fixed and unchanging (Mohanty 2000, 30).

Basing an identity on fixed and unchanging properties provides a significant degree of certainty and clarity. This may explain why so many academics (and nonacademics, for that matter) find essentialist approaches so appealing. However, an essentialist conception of a collective identity can be problematic because the process of establishing this definitional certainty can deny and even threaten the existing internal diversity present in every human social group. Political theorists Clarissa Hayward and Ron Watson outline how critics of the concept of identity characterize this problem. They explain that

> collective identities ... exclude at their boundaries, and internally, they normalize. What is more, working together the universe of recognized identities defines what counts as intelligible ways of living and being, thus rendering unintelligible those who fall within no identity-category. For people who conform, identities serve as mechanisms of power that constrain freedom. For people who do not, they are mechanisms of power that legitimate violence and coercion. (Hayward and Watson 2010, 21–22)

Hayward and Watson argue that an essentialist conception of collective identity can negatively impact peoples' actual lives in two basic ways. First, those who conform may be doing so as a result of group pressure and, even if this pressure is not experienced as coercive by an individual, it is still a limit on human freedom. Second, those who do not conform may be subjected to coercive treatment in order to bring about their compliance or they may be excluded from important social groups. That is, individuals who self-identify as members of a group but who do not tow the "identity line" or who are different in some (unacceptable) way may find that there is no place for them in the group.

This type of social exclusion is troubling because individuals who are left out of important social groups incur significant costs. One cost associated with this type of exclusion is the denial of real, material benefits that are part and parcel of being a member of such a group. This would include a wide range of benefits, such as physical intimacy, financial assistance, the sharing of skills and expertise, and the like. Philosopher Daniel Weinstock (2005, 235) outlines the serious extent of these costs:

> Were I stripped of my membership in an identity-conferring group, I would in some sense be deprived of the reference points and self-understandings around which I organize my everyday existence ... Some memberships, that is, provide us with frameworks within which we lead our lives, rather than pointing towards goals that we set for ourselves in the leading of our lives.

He concludes that the "loss of membership in an identity-conferring group ... is an assault on the very person underlying all possible calculations of benefit and cost" (Weinstock 2005, 235). Weinstock contends that individuals are seriously harmed (psychologically and emotionally) by certain forms of exclusion – harmed to the point, in fact, where standard remedies prescribed by normative theories of justice, such as compensation, become ineffectual.

A number of scholars of Aboriginal politics have incorporated the concerns raised thus far regarding the impact of essentialist approaches in their work on Aboriginal peoples. Good examples include the works of Tim Schouls and Caroline Dick on Aboriginal Canadians, and the work of Manuhuia Barcham on the Maori of New Zealand. According to Schouls (2003, 48), many scholars and practitioners of Aboriginal politics advance conceptualizations of aboriginality that assume that "their [Aboriginal peoples'] identities are largely settled." For Schouls

(2003, 48), this way of approaching aboriginality (wrongly) reduces the study and practice of Aboriginal politics to efforts to (re)write the rules of engagement between Aboriginals and non-Aboriginals in order to more effectively accommodate a fixed collective identity. It obscures from view a number of very important questions and issues that lie at the core of the conflict between Aboriginal and non-Aboriginal Canadians. For example, the question of how aboriginality came to be associated with certain traits in the first place (i.e., the collective identity's evolutionary trajectory), as well as the consequences for Aboriginal peoples of being associated with these traits, are two issues that are generally ignored (Schouls 2003, 48). Scholars such as Rita Dhamoon illustrate that these questions are of particular importance because they turn on the existing power relations between Aboriginal and non-Aboriginal Canadians. According to Dhamoon (2009), these inequitable power relations allow non-Aboriginals to unfairly define both the meaning of aboriginality and the (negative) consequences of holding this collective identity. D'Arcy Vermette's (2008) analysis of a number of important legal cases involving Aboriginal peoples in Canada echoes Dhamoon's basic concerns. Vermette (2008, 22) advances that

> at the outset Aboriginal peoples were excluded from contributing to the original definition of 'Indian.' This is not surprising since it was a term created and imposed by Europeans. Then this word, and the peoples it covers, was placed into an equally exclusive legal process. Therefore, court decisions will undoubtedly produce a definition that has no meaning for those being defined.

For both Dhamoon and Vermette, obscuring power relations from view is counterproductive if the goal is to ameliorate the relationship between Aboriginal and non-Aboriginal peoples.

For his part, Schouls (2003) advances that – instead of relying on essentialist conceptions of aboriginality that base the collective identity on cultural and national traits – aboriginality ought to be conceptualized in a way that incorporates diversity and discussions about the evolution of the collective identity, the implications of holding the identity, and the power relations between members and nonmembers. He sums up his position by arguing that "it is this dimension of flux and process, of ambiguity and complexity, normally associated with relationship building that is missing from the analyses" (Schouls 2003, 48). Addressing these elements is Schouls's way of ensuring that scholars and practitioners do not exclude some of the most fundamental issues associated with the conflict between Aboriginal and non-Aboriginal peoples in Canada.

Barcham's position on approaching the conceptualization of aboriginality also critiques the use of the logic of essentialism. Her concerns centre on the inability of essentialist approaches to adequately account for change and intra-group diversity. According to Barcham (2000, 140), serious repercussions result when the collective identity "is taken as a 'natural' and unproblematic category where in reality it is, as are all identities, socially constructed and historically contingent." Like Schouls, Barcham is concerned that the logic of essentialism negates the inclusion of processes of social transformation and change, which are constitutive aspects of all collective identities. While my analysis of Schouls's work focuses on his argument about the effect of essentialist logic on scholars and practitioners of Aboriginal politics, my analysis of Barcham's work centres on her concern about the impact of essentialist logic on individual members of Aboriginal groups. According to Barcham (2000), an essentialist approach works to deny the internal differences that mark the membership of Aboriginal groups and, as a result, it leads to the marginalization and exclusion of particular (oftentimes vulnerable) group members. Barcham builds this argument through an analysis of the process of extending state recognition to the Maori peoples of New Zealand:

> The atemporality of such official recognitions of difference has led to the reification of certain neotraditional Maori organizational forms to a privileged position wherein they have constituted the definitional means by which Maori are identified as 'authentically' indigenous. While this process has led to the creation of a voice for 'authentic' indigenous claims, it has also led to the coterminous silencing of the 'inauthentic' and the alienation of many Maori people ... The prioritization of identity over difference thus acts to restrict the possible forms that identity can take, as identification becomes a process structured around the recognition

of fixed selves – wherein lived experience is devalued as subordinate to
the idea of an ahistorical ideal of community. (Barcham 2000, 138–39)

Barcham highlights how an essentialized conceptualization of the Maori's
collective identity leads to the silencing and exclusion of those Maori who
do not or cannot identify with the "authentic" Maori way of being (which,
in this instance, is the version of the collective identity put forward by the
neo-traditionalists). Barcham also exposes the ramifications of adopting
this type of conception – namely, ignoring or dismissing the real (though
different) lived experiences of less powerful group members in favour of
an ideal held by other, more powerful group members. Barcham's work
goes some distance to show us how the logic of essentialism produces
exclusion and marginalization.

And there is good reason to believe that this result is not confined to
the case of the Maori. Dick's (2006) analysis of the *Sawridge* dispute
in Canada is illustrative.[3] The *Sawridge* dispute turned on the question of
whether First Nations band councils could deny band membership
to Aboriginal individuals who (re)acquired Indian status in 1985 as a result
of *Bill C-31*.[4] This question was important because prior to 1985, any
Aboriginal woman with Indian status who married out (i.e., married a
man, even an Aboriginal man, without Indian status) lost her status. Loss
of status also generally led to loss of band membership (though this has
now been changed and an individual can now hold the former without
the latter). Contrastingly, Aboriginal men with Indian status who married out did not lose their status, and their wives could become Status
Indians, regardless of whether or not they were Aboriginal. Indian status
is important because it is a prerequisite for qualifying for a number of
federal programs.

The *Sawridge* dispute pitted women who had (re)acquired Indian status
as a result of *Bill C-31* against a number of band councils. In her analysis
of the case, Dick (2006) exposes how the band councils argued that they
had a right to come up with their own membership codes and, in effect,
spell out what it meant to be an Aboriginal member of their community.
The women who had (re)acquired Indian status argued that these membership codes were applied arbitrarily and placed unfair demands on them

and their children, all in the name of upholding a particular understanding of aboriginality. Echoing Barcham, Dick (2006, 113) explains that

> Aboriginal authenticity can further more than one agenda; it can be deployed against those who lack power. The *Sawridge* membership code provides a case in point, operating to exclude reacquired rights women from community membership on the basis of a difference that has been constructed by the forces of colonialism, racism and sexism [that is, by the federal government's rules about Indian status]. Established in the name of preserving the integrity of Aboriginal culture and identity, the Band's membership code serves to perpetuate the gender discrimination first inflicted on Aboriginal women by colonial powers, justify the exclusion of [these] women from community membership, and dominate and oppress those who differ from the authentic Aboriginal norm devised by the community's most powerful members.

Dick's analysis is important for our purposes because it exposes how the logic of essentialism can facilitate the oppression of certain group members. Specifically, when the powerful in the group are able to present their version of the group's identity as authoritative, this can have serious consequences for the less powerful in the group.

Dick, Barcham, and Schouls present compelling critiques of conceptualizations of aboriginality that rely on the logic of essentialism – conceptualizations that would result from the use of traits-based approaches. The list of real-world costs (potentially) triggered by such approaches include facilitating the exclusion and marginalization of vulnerable group members and overlooking existing power relations between and within groups. Taken together, these problems give us good reason to be cautious about employing approaches to identity that are capable of impacting people in such serious ways; in other words, the real-world costs of these approaches can be quite high.

What about relational approaches? Do they result in real-world costs? The short answer is no. The long answer is that the use of relational approaches actually precludes many of the real-world costs cited in the discussion of traits-based approaches. For example, since relational approaches focus on inter-group relations (to some degree) and not on a set of shared traits, they do not require intra-group homogeneity and so do not (necessarily) result in exclusion. Along the same lines, relational approaches do not ignore the significant contingent historical, social, and political factors that play a role in identity formation and maintenance. In many ways, relations are a product of these factors. As a result, relational approaches not only allow for discussions about the evolutionary trajectory and potential of a collective identity, but they appear to require them. And the discussions can provide a solid foundation for empirical analyses of collective identity. More importantly, the discussions expose the existing intra-group and inter-group power relations, which makes it difficult to exclude members of groups or, at the very least, makes it difficult to hide this type of exclusion. When all the advantages of a relational approach are coupled with the fact that the problems resulting from its usage are less morally problematic than the problems associated with the usage of the traits-based approach, we have a solid case for the use of a relational approach.

Conclusion

The argument presented here – that real-world costs are more morally weighty than analytical costs – provides us with the requisite tools for comparing and ranking concepts and theories (at least along one dimension). Because relational approaches result in less harm than traits-based approaches, from this point on, the analysis will be concerned with relational conceptions of aboriginality.

In order to move forward with an analysis of aboriginality and section 35 jurisprudence, it is not enough to know what type of conception of aboriginality to employ. We must also be able to identify different articulations of the collective identity when we come across references to aboriginality in the court material under review. With that in mind, next I turn to the literature on Aboriginal politics and, using a relational approach, construct three different conceptions of aboriginality. These conceptions will make it possible for us to address the following questions when examining the legal material: Did the parties to section 35 litigation present a common version of aboriginality? If not, who advanced which version of aboriginality during section 35 litigation? And how did the Supreme Court of Canada ultimately deal with the multiple versions of the collective identity?

4

The Nation-to-Nation, Colonial, and Citizen-State Approaches

In this chapter, I turn to the scholarly literature on Aboriginal politics to construct three different versions of aboriginality through the use of a relational approach. The goal is to have these versions serve as "ideal types" of the collective identity when we turn to the court material in the following chapters. This chapter is not meant to be an exhaustive analysis of the various conceptualizations of aboriginality found in the scholarship on Aboriginal politics. Those familiar with the Aboriginal political literature will notice some significant omissions; a number of central scholars in the field are treated in a cursory fashion or not at all. Moreover, important traditions are almost entirely unaddressed. The postcolonial and critical theories – as exemplified by the work of scholars such as Taiaiake Alfred (1999) and Lynda Lange (1998), respectively – are probably the most significant of the absent theoretical approaches. The sole consideration in the decision about whose work to include is the presence of similar articulations in both the scholarly literature and the court material. That is, conceptualizations of aboriginality by important groups of scholars were left out only because they did not coincide in any significant way with the versions of aboriginality found in the section 35 factums or judicial rulings.

My approach to the literature relies on a "back-and-forth" dynamic. I created an inventory of conceptualizations of aboriginality found in the literature and then I looked for them in the court material. And while I surveyed the court material, I revised and simplified the conceptualizations of aboriginality in light of the way in which the Aboriginal participants, government representatives, and judges characterized the collective identity.

I eliminated conceptions of aboriginality found in the literature but not in the court material. The final result of this process is three conceptualizations of aboriginality rooted in the scholarship and the court documents.

In this chapter, I focus exclusively on the scholarly roots of these versions of aboriginality. I construct the three versions of this collective identity by drawing on various historical (primarily empirical) and theoretical (primarily normative) patterns of political interaction as described by Aboriginal and non-Aboriginal individuals in the literature. Specifically, first, I organize the sets of political interaction between Aboriginal and non-Aboriginal peoples into paradigms of interaction; second, I extrapolate the requisite characteristics for engaging in these patterns of interaction; and third, I generate a definition of aboriginality that is based on relations that facilitate or allow for these characteristics.

The three definitions of aboriginality generated by this approach are what I call the nation-to-nation, colonial, and citizen-state versions of aboriginality. My decision to use these terms is partially stylistic; I could well have called them conceptions A, B, and C. This decision is also partially strategic; the terms are intended to serve as memory aids for the reader. After all, the modifiers A, B, and C do not tell us very much, whereas the alternatives provide cues to the reader about the contents of each version of aboriginality. I realize that the terms "nation-to-nation" and "colonial" refer to concepts that have received extensive treatments in the scholarly literature. While the versions of aboriginality I outline herein draw on some of these treatments and so share some common conceptual ground (indeed, it is for this reason that I believe that these labels will serve as memory aids), I do not mean for this association to be determinative. Or, stated somewhat more plainly, for my purposes, the definition of each conception of aboriginality that is provided here is complete and the reader should not "read in" additional meaning by drawing on the existing literature. For example, when I employ the phrase "nation-to-nation conception of aboriginality," I mean only what I outline below and not what the broader literature may say about "nation-to-nation" concepts (unless otherwise indicated, of course).

Nation-to-Nation Version of Aboriginality

Scholars from a variety of disciplines advance that during the Encounter era, many Aboriginal peoples and Europeans conducted their political relations on a nation-to-nation basis (Tully 1995; Ladner 2003). For us, the important question is: what types of interactions, specifically, make up a nation-to-nation relationship? The historical scholarship provides some direction. It reveals that during the Encounter era, political interactions between Aboriginals and Europeans were often cooperative and driven by the pursuit of group-specific interests. Aboriginal nations established cooperative relationships with Europeans in order to secure military alliances and gain strategic advantages over their rivals, as well as access to goods from Europe (Williams 1997, 21). Legal scholar Robert Williams (1997, 23) goes so far as to conclude that rather than "being barriers to European expansion, Indians assume[d] essential roles as potential allies and facilitators, acting for their own reasons in concert with European colonial powers." And Europeans had their own motives for acting cooperatively with certain Aboriginal nations:

> Maintaining reliable relationships with powerful tribal groups on their frontiers was essential to the financial success of many of the colonies. The frontier trading tribes controlled the fur supplies and related commerce of the regions bounding the European colonies. They acted as buffers to the expansion and penetration of rival European powers onto that frontier. They could be called on to counter and even war against less cooperative tribes that might be causing difficulties for a colony. (Williams 1997, 25–26)

In many cases, the survival and success of their colonies depended on Europeans' abilities to establish and maintain cooperative relations with their Aboriginal neighbours. Indeed, according to historian J.R. Miller (1989, 40) "the Indian was an indispensable partner ... To preserve fish, to gather fur, to probe and map the land, and to spread the Christian message, cooperation by the Indians was essential."

Scholars also inform us that the establishment and maintenance of cooperative interactions was, in many ways, contingent on recognizing that force was not an effective basis for action. During the Encounter era, a situation of "rough" equality existed between Aboriginal peoples and Europeans. That is, neither Aboriginals nor Europeans were in a position to bring the other fully under their control and both parties recognized this reality (Williams 1997, 21, 25). The absence of clear dominance by either group meant that using coercive force as a means of structuring relations was unlikely to result in success. Recognizing the situation of rough equality facilitated the realization that cooperation based on consent was a more efficient course of action than coercion.[1] The reliance on treaties to structure relations between Aboriginal peoples and Europeans throughout this period is, among other things, evidence of this recognition.

What kind of characteristics would be necessary to engage in cooperative, noncoercive interactions that allow for the pursuit of group-specific interests? Political philosopher James Tully provides a number of important insights regarding the requisite characteristics for engaging in these nation-to-nation interactions. He argues that a party to the nation-to-nation relationship must possess two central features – a recognized equal moral status and the opportunity to actualize this moral status (Tully 1999, 415). According to Tully, equal moral status entitles each party to possess the same moral entitlement to exist as a self-governing nation and to be recognized as such. He goes on to outline the criteria for this type of recognition: A party's status as a self-governing nation is demonstrated by a proven capacity to govern both a people and a territory and to engage in relations ·ith other self-governing parties (Tully 1999, 421). Thus, parties to a 'on-to-nation relationship must recognize each other's self-governing st.   and must order their interactions in such a way as to ensure that this statt. ' maintained.

In   lly's account of a nation-to-nation relationship, all other interactions ι 'ween the parties are structured around negotiations based on reciprocity and consent. Interactions that are a product of negotiations guided by these principles produce significant results. First, interactions arrived at in this fashion (as opposed to coercive force, for example) are a statement about each party's entitlement to govern its people and its territory. Second, by employing these principles, each party is able to exercise its capacity to govern the crucial elements of nationhood. That is, nation-to-nation interactions require that the parties involved be self-governing.

Ovide Mercredi and Mary Ellen Turpel's work on Aboriginal-non-Aboriginal relations brings to the fore another characteristic that parties must possess in order to interact on a nation-to-nation basis. By their account, self-definition is an essential characteristic of nationhood and so of nation-to-nation interaction. "A people who are a nation," they explain, "define themselves" (Mercredi and Turpel 1993, 24–25). Scholars David E. Wilkins and K. Tsianina Lomawaima (2001, 4) concur: "A sovereign nation," they argue, "defines itself and its citizens." The issue is not simply whether the parties to a nation-to-nation relationship ought to share an equivalent moral status (i.e., that each should be regarded as a self-governing nation). Instead, the central concern is who ought to decide the substantive contents of this status. That is, the concern is about who ought to decide what being a member of a particular national group entails. According to these scholars' conceptualizations of the nation-to-nation relationship, each party to the relationship identifies the substantive contents of this status for itself – that is, each party is self-defining. Cooperative, noncoercive interactions that allow for the pursuit of group-specific interests and are informed by acts of mutual recognition constitute the nation-to-nation paradigm of inter-action. In order to engage in these kinds of relations, groups must recognize each other as self-defining nations that are entitled to govern their peoples and territories. Moreover, the process employed to structure the inter-group interactions must take this recognition into account. This means that the principles and procedures that make up this process, and the resulting interactions they generate, must not violate this recognition.

What remains to be determined is an appropriate definition of aborig-inality, where appropriateness hinges on reconciling the meaning of ab-originality with the essential characteristics for engaging in nation-to-nation interactions. When taken together, the various positions regarding the essential characteristics of the parties to a nation-to nation relationship generate just such a portrait of aboriginality. Aboriginality is presented as a collective identity that entails both the recognition of nationhood ac-tualized through the governance of a people and a territory, and the ac-knowledgment that the source of the content of the collective identity is the Aboriginal group itself. Or, stated more plainly, aboriginality of the nation-to-nation variety (at least for our purposes) presupposes relations that facilitate Aboriginal self-government and self-definition.

Colonial Version of Aboriginality

The colonial version of aboriginality is very different from its nation-to-nation counterpart. The differences result from the types of interactions inherent in a colonial relationship. Colonization begins with the involuntary incorporation of a group into a political unit. Thus, the first interaction between the parties is marked by a lack of consent. In a colonial relationship, a lack of consent characterizes not only the initial act of incorporation but also the subsequent interactions between the parties. According to sociologist Robert Blauner (1969, 396), in a colonial relationship, one group is administered by representatives of another group and, as a result, the former experiences being "managed and manipulated by outsiders." Tim Schouls's (2003, 40) account of the relationship that developed between Aboriginal peoples and Europeans in the post-Encounter era illustrates these points in no uncertain terms: "The colonial relationship was a dominant one in which Aboriginal peoples were unilaterally, and without their consent, subject to the superior power and influence of the settler society."

Furthermore, in a colonial relationship, the colonizers often demonstrate a basic disrespect and intolerance toward the social, economic, and political differences that characterize the colonized group. Blauner (1969, 396) describes how "the colonizing power carries out a policy which constrains, transforms, or destroys indigenous values, orientations, and ways of life." In many cases, group difference is based precisely on such things as values, orientations, and ways of life. In essence, colonizing societies attempt to "remake" the members of the colonized group into something else – historically, into mirror images of themselves. A particular set of interactions, which are unilateral in nature and are marked by both a lack of consent and respect for group difference, characterizes the colonial relationship. These interactions are the antithesis of the ones found in the nation-to-nation relationship.

In order to pursue the types of interactions that make up the colonial paradigm, the colonizing party must have both the capacity and the will to do so. In terms of the will to engage in these interactions, political scientist Alan Cairns provides an astute account of the mindset that underpinned colonial interactions between the Canadian state and Aboriginal peoples. He explains that "although non-Aboriginal Canadians would not have described their relation to indigenous peoples in Canada as imperialist, they – if sometimes only unconsciously – had an imperial mentality" (Cairns 2000, 26). Scholar of social justice Sherene Razack (2004, 144) takes a similar position, arguing that "as Canadians we do not see ourselves in imperial history." She goes further than Cairns, however, arguing that this wilful blindness and wilful forgetting underpins contemporary racism in Canada (Razack 1998; 2004).

In any case, this imperial mentality assumed that European societies were at the pinnacle of a hierarchy of civilizations and that Aboriginal societies were at the bottom (Niezen 2003a, 5). This aspect of imperial mentality is outlined in Ronald Niezen's analysis of nineteenth-century comparative studies of human societies:

> For nineteenth century socio-evolutionists, the culture concept answered a need to fit all human societies into a unilineal hierarchy of complexity, sophistication, development and virtue, above all in comparison with (or more precisely, – in contrast to) the pinnacle of human achievement, "civilization." Culture was an extremely broad, "catch-all" concept – covering the entire range of human institutions, values, customs, and practices – that allowed theorists ... to situate human societies on a scale of development, with positive value placed on those aspects of culture that accorded well with European society. (Niezen 2003a, 5)

When assumptions regarding the hierarchical nature of societies combined with a Darwinian conception of competition between different cultures (where superior cultures would win out at the expense of their inferior counterparts), a popular belief developed: Aboriginal peoples would disappear because the surrounding European society would completely assimilate them or because they would die out as a result of the pressures caused by European settlement (Cairns 2000, 40). When non-Aboriginals believed in their cultural and societal superiority, they were able to justify interactions with Aboriginal peoples that were disrespectful and intolerant of Aboriginal difference, unilateral in nature, and marked by a lack of Aboriginal consent. That is, the belief in European (and then later, non-Aboriginal Canadian) superiority underpinned the will to engage in colonial interactions.

In terms of the capacity to engage in colonial interactions, the Canadian state demonstrated, in a myriad of ways, its ability to do so. First, non-Aboriginals conferred upon themselves the power to govern Aboriginal peoples by creating the requisite legal instruments to bring Aboriginal peoples under their jurisdiction. As legal scholar Larry N. Chartrand (2003, 459) points out, "the colonial and Canadian legal systems were not neutral in the 'colonization project.' These legal systems were fully used as tools in the furtherance of colonization goals and in turn became self-justifying principles of law for the continuation and legitimization of colonialism." Once the Canadian state secured the juridical means, it legislated and made policies for Aboriginal peoples. Legal scholar John J. Borrows (2003, 224) cites the "suppression of Aboriginal institutions of government, the denial of land, the forced taking of children, the criminalization of economic pursuits, and the negation of the rights of religious freedom, association, due process and equality," as historical and contemporary examples of government interference and control of Aboriginal peoples, their lands, and their resources. All of this speaks to the Canadian state's capacity to pursue colonial interactions in its dealings with Aboriginal peoples.

For our purposes, nonconsensual, unilateral, and disrespectful inter-actions constitute the colonial paradigm. In order to engage in these types of relations, one of the parties must have the will to do so, and this will is often underpinned by a belief in its own superiority. Moreover, this same party must have the legal and institutional capacity to act. When these conditions are met, and colonial interactions result, a particular version of aboriginality is constructed. In this instance, there is a rejection of self-defining, self-governing nationhood. Aboriginality is understood as a collective identity that is created by persons who do not belong to the group being defined and it denotes the experience of being subject to another people's laws and institutions. Thus, in the analysis that follows, the colonial version of aboriginality entails being defined and ruled by non-Aboriginals.

Citizen-State Version of Aboriginality

Alan Cairns's (2000) concept of "Citizens Plus" is the basis of the citizen-state version of aboriginality. At its core, Citizens Plus is a particular way of conceptualizing (Canadian) citizenship. For many scholars, a hetero-geneous citizenry can pose significant problems for the work and, in some cases, even the continued existence of contemporary liberal democratic states.[2] Cairns develops the Citizens Plus conception of citizenship in order to advance the argument that citizenship (of a certain type) can be a source of unity in an increasingly heterogeneous polity and, thus, can be an effective tool for engaging in collective action and developing feelings of solidarity.

The distinguishing feature of a Citizens Plus view of citizenship is the idea that, under certain circumstances, citizens of a polity should have differentiated rights. Applied to the case of Aboriginal peoples in Canada, this notion of citizenship proposes that they are entitled to the rights and privileges held by all Canadians, as well as an extra bundle of rights not accorded to citizens generally. The purpose of the Citizens Plus concept is to recognize Aboriginal peoples' (ethnocultural) distinctiveness while simultaneously promoting pan-Canadian unity. Cairns (2000, 107) puts forward that, "if the reality is that we are all – Aboriginal and non-Aboriginal alike – massively shaped by cultural and other forces outside our immediate local culture, and if we nevertheless retain separate identities while sharing common values and experiences, we then have a basis for living together and living apart at the same time." This is of primary import, Cairns (2000, 212) concludes, because "both our separateness and our togetherness need to be institutionally supported if the overall Canadian community is to survive."

Citizens Plus is a concept that is concerned with both Aboriginal distinctiveness and pan-Canadian unity. As a result, the citizen-state paradigm envisions two types of interactions: interactions between individuals and their particular bounded communities and interactions between these same individuals and the broader pan-Canadian political community. For Cairns (2000), the former type includes interactions between Aboriginal Canadians and community-level governments (e.g., band councils) or regional and national Aboriginal organizations (e.g., the Union of British Columbia Indian Chiefs or the Congress of Aboriginal Peoples). The latter type includes interactions between Aboriginal peoples and municipal, provincial, and federal governments. The basic argument is that interactions between an Aboriginal individual and Aboriginal governments and organizations allow Aboriginal peoples to maintain their distinctiveness. Interactions between the same individual and municipal, provincial, and federal governments foster a sense of belonging to the pan-Canadian community. According to Cairns (2000), Canadian national unity is the result of successfully balancing these different interactions.

Feelings of attachment are necessary in order to engage in these two types of interaction. Cairns's concept of Citizens Plus entails a concern for membership in and attachment to both a particular bounded community (the Aboriginal component of belonging) and a broader political community (the pan-Canadian dimension of belonging). What comes to the fore is the importance this concept places on both types of attachment. From the Citizens Plus view, these bonds of attachment are so important, in fact, that they merit legal and constitutional protection. Group-specific rights protect the bonds of attachment to Aboriginal communities, while a common regime of citizenship and rights facilitates feelings of solidarity to the broader pan-Canadian political community (Cairns 2000, 157).

The final component of the citizen-state version of aboriginality relates to the issue of sovereignty. While Cairns's concept of Citizens Plus does not necessarily exclude the possibility of some degree of self-government for Aboriginal peoples, given his rejection of parallelism/treaty federalism,[3] it is not unreasonable to conclude that Citizens Plus does not advance a form of self-government that challenges the underlying sovereignty of the Canadian Crown (Cairns 2000, 115, 157–58). The significant role played by a common regime of citizenship and rights in Cairns's characterization of the Citizens Plus concept indicates that the opposite is, in fact, the case. After all, from this view, Canadian citizenship and rights (both the common rights held by all Canadians and the "special" rights held only by Aboriginal Canadians) are the products of the sovereignty of the Crown, and it is through this sovereignty that they are protected. According to Native American studies scholar Dale Turner (2006, 57), Cairns holds that sovereignty in Canada is divided solely between the federal and provincial governments. In this regard, Marc Hanvelt and Martin Papillon (2005, 249) are correct to conclude that "Cairns never questions the basis for the legitimacy of Canada's sovereignty over Aboriginal peoples." As a result, acceptance of the sovereignty of the Crown is also a necessary component of citizen-state interactions as described here.

The citizen-state conception of aboriginality advanced in this work can be characterized as following: When aboriginality is constructed within the citizen-state paradigm of interaction, it is understood as a single component, or facet, of an individual's overall identity. This important aspect of the individual's overall identity denotes a connection with a particular

Aboriginal community. It exists in concert with another significant facet – membership in a broader pan-Canadian political community where the Crown is sovereign. Aboriginal rights protect the former facet of the individual's overall identity, while Canadian citizenship and rights protect the latter facet.

Conclusion

Each of the three conceptualizations of aboriginality envisions different political relations between Aboriginal and non-Aboriginal people. The nation-to-nation version of aboriginality is based on relations that allow for Aboriginal self-government and self-definition; the colonial version is based on relations that allow for external (i.e., non-Aboriginal) definition and rule by non-Aboriginals; and the citizen-state version is concerned with relations that balance attachments to Aboriginal communities and the broader pan-Canadian community.

As will become evident in the following chapters, these three conceptions play a significant role in the construction of Aboriginal rights in Canada. When section 35 cases have been before the courts (from 1990 to 2014), the Aboriginal litigants, the federal and provincial governments, and the justices of the Supreme Court of Canada have advanced these three different conceptions of aboriginality by supporting differing views about the types of interactions that ought to underpin the Aboriginal-non-Aboriginal relationship. The lack of agreement over the meaning of the Aboriginal collective identity impacts Aboriginal rights and, more importantly, Aboriginal peoples in Canada.

5

Submissions to the Court

Disagreement about what aboriginality means is, indeed, a very real possibility when scholars employ the term "Aboriginal." Thus far, the analysis has offered very little by way of specifics about this debate about how to conceptualize aboriginality and Aboriginal rights. By focusing on the case of Aboriginal rights litigation in Canada, the remainder of this book assesses the ramifications of this type of disagreement on an actual political conflict. This chapter traces the conceptions of aboriginality presented to the Supreme Court of Canada (SCC) by the federal and provincial attorneys general and the Aboriginal participants involved in section 35 litigation. The analysis is based on the participants' factums from sixteen section 35 cases between 1990 and 2014. During this period, the attorneys general and the Aboriginal participants advanced two different conceptions of aboriginality, illustrating that definitional contestation is, indeed, a live factor in Aboriginal rights litigation in Canada.

Aboriginality According to the Aboriginal Participants

Between 1990 and 2014, Aboriginal peoples participated in section 35 cases as both litigants and interveners. They represent a wide range of Aboriginal organizations, communities, and nations. Culture, religion, geography, economic conditions, and many other factors distinguish these participants in significant ways. That having been said, an examination of the factums submitted by all of the Aboriginal participants reveals substantial commonality regarding the way in which they characterize aboriginality. The Aboriginal litigants and interveners argue that their relationship with non-Aboriginals should allow for self-definition and self-government. For the Aboriginal litigants, this is how collectives like theirs should be treated. In short, they advance a nation-to-nation conception of aboriginality.

Self-Definition

Given that the SCC decided that the purpose of section 35 is to protect aboriginality, it is perhaps not surprising that most of the Aboriginal participants in the cases under review included characterizations of aboriginality in their legal submissions to the court. In instances where an Aboriginal nation described itself, these are of course instances of self-definition. What is of import for this analysis is not only that Aboriginal nations included in their section 35 factums their own understandings of aboriginality, but the type of understandings they advanced. Specifically, Aboriginal participants often drew constitutive links between aboriginality and important interests that came up during section 35 litigation. In other words, they argued that those interests were not just important for the protection of aboriginality, they were constitutive of aboriginality. Aboriginality, as they described it, was made up of those interests. If we examine the way in which Aboriginal participants talked about natural resources, territory, and conceptions of the good (or worldviews), we can see this process of self-definition at work.

Since 1990, the SSC has ruled on numerous cases relating to natural resources.[1] In these cases, Aboriginal participants have argued, time and time again, that there is an important link between aboriginality and the bounty of the natural world. Specifically, the former is said to be determined, in significant ways, by the latter. For example, in the *Sparrow* case, the appellant Ronald E. Sparrow argued that salmon and salmon fishing have always been central parts of the Musqueam nation's culture.[2] Intervening in this case, the Assembly of First Nations (AFN) provided a characterization of the Musqueam nation that supported Sparrow's claim. This organization's factum advanced that the Musqueam "identity and survival as distinct peoples is linked to the salmon."[3] What these statements share is the contention that this natural resource occupies a central role in the characterization of the Aboriginal nation's collective identity and culture.

A similar argument was submitted by the Aboriginal appellant in the *Van der Peet* case. According to Dorothy Van der Peet, the Fraser River plays a direct role in the structure of Stó:lō society and the Stó:lō people's sense of collective identity. She stated in her factum that "Sto:lo means 'people of the river' and ... [the fact that] all the Sto:lo villages in the past and today are located along the Fraser River and its tributaries attests to the centrality of the fishing to Sto:lo social organization."[4] She went on to say that "the river and its resources are the very definition of the people."[5] The Fraser River and the salmon were presented as integral parts of what it means to be Stó:lō.

The factums submitted by Aboriginal participants for consideration in the *Sparrow* and *Van der Peet* cases reveal something quite important about the link between aboriginality and natural resources. The Aboriginal participants advanced that natural resources are more than incidental descriptors of the collective identities of the Stó:lō and Musqueam. They argued that these elements are constitutive and fundamental – that is, they are central elements of these nations' collective identities. The implication is that without these elements, any characterization of their collective identities would be incomplete and unintelligible to those who bear them.

Moreover, Aboriginal participants in section 35 cases have made similar types of claims about the link between aboriginality and traditional territories. For example, the Wet'suwet'n appellants in the *Delgamuukw* case put forward that their society is organized around three foundational institutions – the House, the Clan, and the Feast – that are linked to territory in important ways.[6] They outlined how the Wet'suwet'en are organized into territorially based Houses and Clans, then argued that identifying as a member of a House and Clan includes, by definition, identifying with a certain territory.[7] For this reason, the appellants concluded that the "proprietary relationship between House, Chief and territory is an integral part of the organization, culture, laws, and ceremonies which define Wet'suwet'en identity."[8]

A number of the self-characterizations outlined in the factums submitted in the *Delgamuukw* and *Van der Peet* cases included views about Aboriginal conceptions of the good. Just like natural resources and traditional territories, conceptions of the good were presented by the Aboriginal participants as constitutive elements of their sense of their collective identities. For example, in the *Delgamuukw* case, the Gitksan Hereditary Chiefs (the other Aboriginal appellants in the case) advanced the notion that their laws and land tenure system are underpinned by a particular worldview. This worldview is based on the belief that the members of their Aboriginal nation are stewards of the claimed land and, as such, must engage in respectful land management and resource exploitation.[9] Moreover, the Hereditary Chiefs made the argument that this conception of the good ought to be incorporated in the court's final ruling (i.e., that it ought to be included in the construction of section 35 rights). This is evident if one examines the appellants' proposed construction of the concept of Aboriginal title. The Gitksan put forward that "Aboriginal title ... carries with it a right to maintain their [the Gitksan] stewardship over, and their spiritual and material relationship with those [claimed] lands."[10] This highlights the Gitksan position that the members of that nation see themselves as the rightful stewards of the disputed territory, and this view underpins their claim that the court's construction of Aboriginal title ought to facilitate the continuation of this stewardship.

A similar claim was expressed by the Stó:lō appellant in the *Van der Peet* case. According to the appellant, Stó:lō oral history describes "an ancient respectful and spiritual relationship between the Sto:lo, the salmon and the Fraser River."[11] This relationship, like the one outlined by the Gitksan Chiefs, is best characterized as a form of stewardship. The appellant's factum in the *Van der Peet* case also included an obligation to ensure that this relationship would be protected for future generations. The factum put forward that the "Sto:lo believe that the Creator gave the Sto:lo the responsibility to take care of the fishery within their territory and to harvest fish for the benefit of this generation and for generations unborn."[12] This statement mirrors the obligation identified by the Gitksan Hereditary Chiefs. In fact, there is a parallel between the position taken by the Stó:lō in regard to the inclusion of Aboriginal conceptions of the good in the construction of section 35 rights and the position taken by the Gitksan on this same issue. "Fishing rights," Van der Peet argued, "are more closely defined as the relationship of the Sto:lo to the Creator, to the fish, to the fishery and to each other, their ancestors and generations unborn. The right embraces the laws, and the accumulated knowledge of the fishery to this generation, who in turn are expected to teach the next."[13] Van der Peet made the case to the court that section 35 rights should facilitate Stó:lō stewardship over the fishery.

Stó:lō and Gitksan conceptions of the good underpin the way in which these Aboriginal nations define themselves. They are the stewards of this territory or that natural resource. These Aboriginal nations describe the existence of a unique relationship based on the principle of stewardship between the members of their nations and the natural world. The views expressed above reveal that that vision not only influences how the nations define themselves, but it also impacts their positions regarding the ultimate scope of the rights that they believe are capable of protecting their collective identities. That is, the ways in which the Aboriginal nations characterize aboriginality underpin the Aboriginal parties' positions regarding what section 35 rights should entail.

Self-Government

The factums submitted to the court by the Aboriginal participants contained a multipropositional argument about self-government, generally outlined as follows. First, all of the Aboriginal parties described their specific communities (or Aboriginal peoples in general) as self-governing nations. Second, the participants supported this view by taking the position that Aboriginal self-government is linked in significant ways to Aboriginal culture and identity. And third, the participants concluded that nation-to-nation negotiations and treaty making are the proper mechanisms for structuring relations between Aboriginal peoples and the Canadian state.

In their submissions to the SCC, numerous Aboriginal parties described Aboriginal nations (and their historical counterparts) either as self-governing political entities or as political entities that are entitled to powers of self-government. In the *Sparrow* case, intervening on behalf of the appellant, the Assembly of First Nations (AFN) characterized the original Aboriginal inhabitants of North America as "organized in distinct and self-governing societies."[14] In the *Delgamuukw* case, the Gitksan appellants argued that their nation has "an unextinguished right to self-government."[15] In the same case, the Wet'suwet'en appellants stated that "they have certain rights which may be described as rights of 'governance,' in that they concern the role of traditional laws and structures of governance in relation to the territory and the land."[16] In all of these factums, self-government or powers associated with governing were deployed in the characterizations of aboriginality.

In the case of *R. v. Pamajewon*,[17] the Federation of Saskatchewan Indians (FSI) and White Bear First Nations (WBFN), intervening on behalf of the Aboriginal appellants, echoed these sentiments regarding Aboriginal rights of governance.[18] The FSI and WBFN, however, offered an important clarification. They insisted that Aboriginal self-government rights "do not owe their existence to particular legislation or Crown grant."[19] Factums submitted by Aboriginal participants in section 35 cases identified two sources for this right to self-government: Aboriginal societies and Aboriginal occupation of land. The Westbank First Nation (WFN) advanced the former position in its submission to the court during the *Delgamuukw* case.[20] The Aboriginal appellants in the *Pamajewon* case put forward the latter position, arguing that the right of self-government "is an inherent right flowing from their peoples' history in their homelands."[21] The FSI and WBFN concurred with the appellants' explanation, citing as the source of Aboriginal rights of governance the fact that "First Nations were living in what is now Canada and governing their own peoples prior to contact."[22] In all of these submissions to the court relating to self-government, the Aboriginal participants argued that Aboriginal nations are self-governing entities that have rights of governance that result from historical occupation of the land and/or an organized society.

In many instances, the Aboriginal factums advanced the argument that Aboriginal self-government is exercised through institutions that are not only institutions of governance but are also significant cultural institutions. These institutions were identified as mechanisms for the maintenance of Aboriginal identity. For example, in the *Delgamuukw* case, the Gitksan Hereditary Chiefs insisted that "the means and exercise of self-government within aboriginal society is a characteristic of such society no less integral to its distinctive culture than its language, spirituality, resource use or ancestral homelands."[23] From this view, the means and exercise of self-government are presented as significant markers of cultural distinctiveness and as constitutive elements of Aboriginal culture. The importance of the exercise of self-government is revealed by the fact that a parallel is drawn between self-government and some commonly cited markers of culture and collective identity – that is, language, religion, and territory.

The factums of the Aboriginal participants also included several references to treaty making as the appropriate way to conduct relations between

Aboriginal peoples and the Canadian state. In *R. v. Pamajewon*, the appellants contended that the basic "premise of aboriginal rights is that the Crown and aboriginal peoples will exercise their respective rights and responsibilities in an arrangement which reconciles their mutual and competing interests."[24] The Aboriginal appellants went on to clarify that the "Courts have never sought to define the actual terms of that arrangement. That was the task of negotiated treaties."[25] The appellants advanced an important normative claim – namely, that the basic rules of engagement for Aboriginal-Crown interactions (i.e., each party's rights and responsibilities) ought to be worked out vis-à-vis negotiations and treaty making.

The AFN's intervention in the case of *R. v. Sparrow* provided a historical explanation for this normative claim (and the existing Aboriginal emphasis on treaty making). According to the AFN, historically, Aboriginal peoples and the Crown relied on treaty making in order to structure their relations with one another. The AFN pointed to the alienation of Aboriginal lands as a prime example, explaining that it could only result from the treaty-making process.[26] On that basis, the AFN concluded that "by the treaties, the Crown recognized the Indian tribes or nations as polities."[27] From this view, the treaty-making process is important not only because it is a model for structuring Aboriginal-Crown relations; it is also significant because it constitutes a form of recognition of Aboriginal nationhood.

The factums submitted by the Aboriginal participants involved in section 35 litigation included both significant examples of self-definition and references to self-government. The examples of self-definition presented thus far reveal two things of import. First, they expose that, even though these factums were produced by members of different Aboriginal nations, the participants employed common substantive components in their characterizations of aboriginality. The common components included the relationship between Aboriginal peoples and the natural world (including land and resources) and Aboriginal conceptions of the good.

The various references to self-government found within the factums worked to present the argument that aboriginality entails self-governing nationhood. This was accomplished, first, by arguing that Aboriginal nations are entitled to self-government and/or powers of self-government. Second, a substantial link between Aboriginal culture and self-government (both its exercise and its form) was drawn. This link acted to render the exercise of self-government a constitutive aspect of aboriginality. Moreover, negotiations and treaty making were held as the appropriate mechanisms for dealing with these self-governing nations. In short, the factums submitted by Aboriginal participants in these cases presented a characterization of aboriginality that entails self-defining, self-governing nationhood. Over the past two decades, Aboriginal participants in Aboriginal rights cases – both litigants and interveners – have consistently presented a nation-to-nation understanding of aboriginality in their submissions to the court.

Aboriginality According to the Federal and Provincial Governments

The attorneys general (AGs) involved in section 35 cases between 1990 and 2014 represented different federal and provincial governments. Unlike the Aboriginal participants, they presented no consensus position on aboriginality in the government factums. Instead, they presented two distinct positions. The first position, which was advanced by most AGs in the early to mid-1990s, is the focus of this chapter. It is premised on two features: external (i.e., non-Aboriginal) definition of aboriginality and external rule of Aboriginal peoples. In short, the AGs advanced a colonial conception of aboriginality as their original position in section 35 litigation. However, by the late 1990s, a number of AGs began to advance a different characterization of aboriginality – a citizen-state conception, which had been first outlined by the SCC. This second characterization is the focus of Chapter 6. Both conceptions of aboriginality are still used by the AGs in section 35 litigation, though the second characterization has become more common than the first.

External Definitions of Aboriginality

A key element of the original characterization of aboriginality advanced by the AGs is that aboriginality can be defined by non-Aboriginals. There are numerous instances in the section 35 legal material in which both federal and provincial AGs rejected Aboriginal participants' self-definitions and presented their own versions of aboriginality. For example, in the case of *R. v. Sparrow*, the AG of Canada advanced that fishing, as of the 1960s, was no longer a significant element of Musqueam culture.[28] The AG went so far as to argue that "the Band had practically turned its back to the sea

for food fishing purposes and that the fishing that did occur bore no re-
semblance whatsoever to the historical intensity level, purpose and mode
of exploitation by the ancient Musqueam."[29] In the same case, the AG of
British Columbia reinforced the AG of Canada's position by contending
that the Indian food fishery was a creation of legislation.[30] Taken together,
these submissions represented a rejection of the argument advanced by the
Aboriginal participants that the fishery is of central importance to the
Musqueam people's identity and culture. Moreover, the government submissions attempted to establish that the fishery is, in actual fact, a product
of Crown legislation, making it impossible for the fishery to be a constitutive
aspect of the Aboriginal nation's collective identity, as the Aboriginal litigants had claimed.

Unlike in the *Sparrow* case, in *R. v. Van der Peet,* the role that food
fishing played in Stó:lō culture was not at issue. Instead, the Crown attempted to make the case (contra the Aboriginal litigant's claim) that the
historical Stó:lō trade of fish was not commercial in nature.[31] The Crown
offered the following explanation:

> Food, wealth, and access to resources were exchanged within the family,
> and with other families connected through ties of kinship and marriage,
> on the basis of reciprocity. The social exchange was not a market system.
> There was no all-purpose money. It was not possible to take a surplus of
> food and simply peddle it. One had to have the social relations that made
> exchange possible. The economy was therefore firmly embedded in the
> social networks.[32]

Similarly, in *Gladstone,* the Crown put forward the argument that the
Heiltsuk did not traditionally participate in commercial trading of herring
spawn on kelp.[33] The Crown stated that "trading herring spawn on kelp
was not a major feature of the culture of the Heiltsuk Band."[34]

In both of these cases, the Aboriginal appellants assigned significant
weight to resource exploitation and trade in their self-characterizations.
In other words, the appellants described their collective identities in reference to these activities. By rejecting the validity of these connections
(i.e., by denying that the Stó:lō and the Heiltsuk actually harvested and
traded these resources commercially), the representatives of the Crown

rejected, in essence, the Stó:lō and Heiltsuk characterizations of their collective identities. This left space for the same Crown representatives to offer their own characterizations of the Aboriginal identities. In *Van der Peet*, for example, the Crown characterized the Stó:lō not as commercial traders, but as social traders (i.e., people who engage in trade in order to maintain social and kinship connections). This characterization of the Stó:lō is, indeed, markedly different from the one advanced by the Stó:lō themselves.

In the *Pamajewon* and *Delgamuukw* cases, a similar dynamic of rejection and external definition was at work. In the former case, the AG of Ontario stated that "Bingo has nothing to do with the culture, practices or history of the Shawanaga people ... Casinos and commercial destination gambling are foreign to the culture, practices and history of the Shawanaga. These are European in origin."[35] The AG advanced the position that the practices of gambling at issue in the case are elements of European cultures and, as a result, cannot be elements of the Shawanaga nation's culture. In short, for the AG of Ontario, practices that are European cannot also be Aboriginal.

In the *Delgamuukw* case, the Wet'suwet'en and Gitksan appellants advanced that traditional territories are a central component of their nations' social organization, culture, laws, and collective identity.[36] The AG of Canada, again, rejected the appellants' positions. First, the AG challenged the appellants' view of the dimensions of their traditional territories and the role that the territories played in the formation and maintenance of their collective identities by advancing that "the evidence does not establish that, at contact and excluding the effects of the commercial fur trade, the appellants' ancestors occupied lands outside the immediate areas of the villages for purposes that were integral to the distinctive culture of their societies."[37] The AG went on to challenge the notion that the appellants' laws and customs governed the territories. The AG submitted that the "trial judge found that what the appellants' witnesses described as law was really 'a most uncertain and highly flexible set of customs which are frequently not followed by the Indians themselves.' This conclusion was entirely justified on the evidence."[38] Once again, the dynamic of rejection and replacement is evident. The AG of Canada rejected the Aboriginal appellants' characterizations of the size and identity-related roles of traditional territories and then proceeded to offer an alternative account of the issues. The AG's position was, basically, that outside of the Wet'suwet'en and Gitksan village sites, land was ungoverned and had no significant relationship with aboriginality.

External Rule of Aboriginal Peoples

In the *Delgamuukw* case, the submissions made by the AG of British Columbia regarding the issue of Aboriginal self-government also included this dynamic of rejection and replacement. While the Wet'suwet'en and Gitksan appellants characterized their claims as rights of self-government, the AG of British Columbia characterized the governing powers of Aboriginal nations as powers of self-regulation. The AG of British Columbia argued that "a self-government right is a right in the aboriginal community to regulate or govern its members inter se [among themselves]. It is properly described as 'self' (or 'internal') in that it does not permit the governance or regulation of non-members."[39] The AG explained that "the defining feature of the right of self-government is that it recognizes the aboriginal community's right or power to govern its members by the creation and enforcement of norms of behaviour or conduct in accordance with historical customs, practices and traditions."[40] Self-government constructed in this fashion institutes social norms that aim to govern the social behaviour of members of an Aboriginal community. It does not entail the right to institute laws that apply to nonmembers or laws that would regulate nonsocial activities (e.g., land and natural resource regulations). This understanding is very different from the claim of jurisdiction and self-government advanced by the Aboriginal litigants, who took the position that self-government includes the capacity to make laws in relation to a broad spectrum of matters, including land.[41] The argument made by the AG of British Columbia hinged on the proposition that aboriginality entitles Aboriginal people to a right more properly understood as a right of self-regulation, not a right of self-government. Thus, the AG of British Columbia also advanced a very different version of aboriginality than the one put forward by the Aboriginal appellants.

The colonial version of aboriginality not only entails instances of external definition, but it also includes the notion that Aboriginal peoples are subject to the rule of others (i.e., non-Aboriginals). Indeed, federal and provincial

AGs put forward claims of this nature in a number of submissions to the court. For example, in the *Gladstone* case, the AG of Alberta argued that "there is no broad right of self-government or self-regulation that would enable the Heiltsuk to reject the concept of a licensing scheme."[42] That is, the provincial intervener explicitly stated that the Aboriginal nation does not possess rights of self-government or self-regulation that would render it exempt from the government's existing regulatory system. Similarly, in the *Delgamuukw* case, the AG of British Columbia advanced that underlying title to the land, and the capacity to govern that land, is vested in the Crown. The AG put forward that "pre-Confederation laws are clearly inconsistent with, and hence extinguish, an aboriginal land tenure system which purports to vest in the aboriginal community a title that would burden the Crown's title. There could only be one legal system which creates interest in land and as of sovereignty that legal system was that of the Colony of BC."[43] From this view, since the Crown's assertion of sovereignty, there was to be room for only one legal order in what became Canada, and that legal order was the non-Aboriginal one. From that time on, Aboriginal peoples and their lands were to be governed by this, and only this, legal order.

Similarly, in the *Pamajewon* case, the AG of Ontario rejected the position that the Shawanaga and Eagle Lake First Nations have a right to conduct high-stakes gaming on their reserves, or (more importantly) have the capacity to legislate any matters relating to criminal law. Referring to section 91(24) of the *Constitution Act, 1867*, the AG argued that "the intention of the Crown to extinguish the right of self-government of the Shawanaga First Nation or the larger aboriginal nation to which the Shawanaga First Nation belongs or belonged at the relevant time has been clearly and plainly expressed. This necessarily includes criminal law making capacity."[44] These First Nations were presented as lacking the right to regulate gaming on their reserves because these matters, the First Nations in question, and their reserve lands are all under the jurisdiction of the federal government. This position is quite different from one that advances that the First Nations are self-governing peoples.

In the *Sparrow* case, the AG of Alberta accepted the notion that Aboriginal peoples have collective rights but defined them in such a way as to make the nations subject to the overarching authority of the Crown. By overarching authority, I mean that the Crown's authority is not limited by the rights in question. The AG of Alberta explained that "Indians were considered to have certain limited rights, described as usufructuary rights dependent on the goodwill of the Crown."[45] In this case, two important points speak to the notion that Aboriginal peoples are subject to the complete rule of outsiders. First, usufructuary rights allow an individual or group to use and enjoy the benefits of land in the absence of possession of underlying title to that land. Title rests not with the holders of the rights but with others (in this case, the Crown). Second, the insistence that Aboriginal peoples' rights exist at the pleasure of the Crown means that these rights may be infringed at the Crown's discretion. Both of these conditions work to explain how one can make the statement that a group possesses rights and simultaneously say that the same group is under the authority of another.

By far the clearest example of the argument that Aboriginal nations are subject to non-Aboriginal rule comes in the form of claims by the AGs about the ultimate sovereignty of the Crown. In the case of *Mitchell v. M.N.R.*, the appellant, the minister of national revenue, argued that the Aboriginal litigants did not possess the right to cross Canada's international border with the United States without paying duties, because such a right would be irreconcilable with Canadian sovereignty.[46] The minister submitted that "Canadian sovereignty entails the power to control both who and what enters the country."[47] From this view, the Aboriginal litigants were subject to the sovereignty of the Crown and, as a consequence, could not cross the international border without being subject to the Crown's existing rules and regulations.

Similarly, in the *Pamajewon* case, the AG of Canada argued that "a[n aboriginal] claim to sovereignty cannot be supported at Canadian law."[48] The AG went on to state that "Canadian sovereignty is a legal reality recognized by the law of nations. This court in *R. v. Sparrow*, rejected the notion that the aboriginal peoples of Canada might retain any measure of sovereignty."[49] According to the AG of Canada, the important point to take away from this position is that, in what is now Canada, the Crown is sovereign and Aboriginal peoples are subject to that sovereignty.

Conclusion

This chapter examines what the Aboriginal participants and some federal and provincial AGs said about aboriginality when they found themselves face-to-face in court. The analysis in this chapter employs a relational approach to identity and, thus, focuses on the specific relations identified by each party as constitutive aspects of the Aboriginal collective identity. The analysis demonstrates that for the Aboriginal participants, self-definition and self-rule are constitutive characteristics of aboriginality. In other words, they advanced a nation-to-nation conception of aboriginality in section 35 litigation. Contrastingly, for the AGs (especially early on in section 35 litigation), external definition and external rule are constitutive. The government representatives advanced a colonial conception during litigation. Over the course of two decades of section 35 litigation, Aboriginal participants and government representatives held different conceptions of aboriginality. What remains to be seen is what the SCC had to say about that collective identity.

6

What the Justices Said

In the case of *R. v. Van der Peet*, Chief Justice Lamer advanced that Aboriginal rights "arise from the fact that aboriginal people are aboriginal."[1] For Chief Justice Lamer, "aboriginal rights 'inhere in the very meaning of aboriginality.' "[2] If Aboriginal rights inhere in the very meaning of aboriginality, then it is important to examine what the justices of the Supreme Court of Canada (SCC) said in section 35 jurisprudence about the nature and scope of Aboriginal rights to understand their characterization of aboriginality. And so, we turn again to the jurisprudence on section 35 and its corresponding academic commentary.

In their decisions, the justices of the SCC identified attachments to Aboriginal communities and to the pan-Canadian political community as fundamental aspects of an Aboriginal identity. Critical academic commentary on section 35 reveals that section 35 rights do, indeed, aim to protect aboriginality by protecting these two types of attachment. In short, this chapter illustrates that, rather than adopt a nation-to-nation conception of aboriginality (as advanced by the Aboriginal participants) or a colonial conception (as advanced by many attorneys general), the justices of the SCC put forward a citizen-state conception of that collective identity.

Attachment to an Aboriginal Community

According to the SCC, how does section 35 protect an Aboriginal person's attachment to an Aboriginal community? An analysis of the Aboriginal rights jurisprudence shows that the protection is achieved by protecting two key aspects of an Aboriginal community – culture and territory. Section 35 rights assist Aboriginal people to continue their attachments to Aboriginal communities because these rights protect Aboriginal cultures and traditional territories. In this chapter, I identify where the court outlines this relationship between Aboriginal rights, culture, and territory by analyzing the doctrine of Aboriginal rights, the tests for Aboriginal activity-based rights, and Aboriginal title. The analysis also exposes the unique and substantive links between Aboriginal cultures and territories envisioned by the court. Specifically, for the SCC, the links are of such importance that a significant amount of the rationale for protecting Aboriginal territories (vis-à-vis the extension of Aboriginal title) turns on concerns about Aboriginal culture.

The analysis begins with the doctrine of Aboriginal rights, the court's explanation of the purpose and functions of section 35. In the case of *R. v. Van der Peet*, Chief Justice Lamer described the doctrine of Aboriginal rights in the following way:

> The doctrine of aboriginal rights exists ... because of one simple fact: when Europeans arrived in North America, aboriginal peoples were already here, living in communities on the land, and participating in distinctive cultures, as they had done for centuries. It is this fact, and this fact above all others, which separates aboriginal peoples from all other minority groups in Canadian society and which mandates their special legal, and now constitutional status.[3]

In this iteration of the doctrine of Aboriginal rights, the facts of prior social organization, distinctive cultures, and lands are, first, factors that distinguish Aboriginal Canadians from non-Aboriginal Canadians and, second, aspects of the collective identity of Aboriginal peoples that merit a particular legal and constitutional status. For all intents and purposes, then, these aspects of aboriginality are legally and constitutionally significant. That is, for the SCC, these are the legally relevant constitutive elements of its characterization of aboriginality.

The test for identifying Aboriginal rights developed by the court supports this proposition. Chief Justice Lamer stated that "[the test] must aim at identifying the practices, traditions and customs central to the aboriginal societies that existed in North America prior to contact with the

Europeans."[4] He went on to conclude that "identifying those practices, traditions and customs that are integral to distinctive aboriginal cultures will serve to identify the crucial elements of the distinctive aboriginal societies that occupied North America prior to the arrival of Europeans."[5] Consequently, the test for Aboriginal rights hinges on practices, customs, and traditions that are integral to the distinctive pre-contact cultures of Aboriginal peoples and that are crucial elements of distinctive pre-contact Aboriginal societies. By protecting these distinctive and integral elements of Aboriginal culture, the court contends that it is, thus, protecting Aboriginal groups. One could say that, from this view, Aboriginal peoples are accommodated by the Canadian legal-political structure because they have the requisite constitutional means to maintain their attachment to these cultural groups.

The test for Aboriginal rights, as formulated by the SCC, centres on a concern for protecting aboriginality by extending protection to identifiable and discrete practices, traditions, and customs that constitute the collective identity. Not all Aboriginal practices, traditions, and customs are candidates for constitutional protection. In the 2001 case of *Mitchell v. M.N.R.*, Chief Justice McLachlin (the current chief justice) outlined how to identify the aspects of Aboriginal culture that are candidates for protection. Chief Justice McLachlin stated that the "practice, tradition or custom must have been integral to the distinctive culture of the aboriginal people in the sense that it distinguished or characterized their traditional culture and lay at the core of the aboriginal people's identity."[6] Chief Justice McLachlin clarified that "it [the activity] must be a 'defining feature' of the aboriginal society, such that the culture would be 'fundamentally altered' without it ... This excludes practices, traditions and customs that are only marginal or incidental to the aboriginal society's cultural identity, and emphasizes practices, traditions and customs that are vital to the life, culture and identity of the aboriginal society."[7] As we can see from the chief justice's explanation, Aboriginal rights protect the practices, customs, and traditions that constitute (in the sense of distinguishing) a particular Aboriginal culture. And this cultural protection is the means for protecting Aboriginal peoples' attachments to their communities.

The SCC's characterization of Metis section 35 rights, two years after the *Mitchell* case, was in many respects a restatement of this position. In

R. v. Powley, the SCC reasoned that "the purpose and the promise of s.35(1) is to protect practices that persist in the present day as integral elements of their Metis culture."[8] Again, the main consideration here, as in the cases that came before *Powley*, was the idea that section 35 rights (be they rights held by First Nations or Metis nations) aim to accommodate Aboriginal peoples by affording Aboriginal cultural activities certain protections.

Aside from being distinctive and integral, Aboriginal cultural activities must also be compatible with the sovereignty of the Crown. In its *Sparrow* ruling, the SCC included a forceful and unambiguous statement about the nature of the Crown's sovereignty. The SCC put forward that "there was from the outset never any doubt that sovereignty and legislative power, and indeed underlying title ... vests in the Crown."[9] The court highlighted the importance of the Crown's sovereignty by stating quite unambiguously that it is not subject to any doubt. Given the SCC's position regarding the importance of the Crown's sovereignty, it is easy to see how considerations regarding the sovereignty of the Crown made it into the SCC's construction of section 35, as well as the version of aboriginality that the constitutional provision is meant to protect.

Years later, Chief Justice Lamer, writing for the majority in the *Van der Peet* case, provided an indication of the manner in which the doctrine of Aboriginal rights balances concerns about Aboriginal attachment to particular Aboriginal communities with issues that "bump up against" the sovereignty of the Crown:

> What s.35(1) does is provide the constitutional framework through which the fact that aboriginals lived on the land in distinctive societies, with their own practices, traditions and cultures, is acknowledged and reconciled with the sovereignty of the Crown. The substantive rights which fall within the provision must be defined in light of this purpose; the aboriginal rights recognized and affirmed by s.35(1) must be directed towards the reconciliation of the pre-existence of aboriginal societies with the sovereignty of the Crown.[10]

The court advanced the argument that only those attachments to an Aboriginal community that can be reconciled with the sovereignty of the Crown are candidates for constitutional protection. By way of contrast, an attachment of this type that cannot be reconciled with the Crown's sovereignty cannot be a constitutive aspect of the justices' conception of aboriginality. This last point is reinforced by the fact that the aforementioned aspects would not be covered by the doctrine of Aboriginal rights and so, to use Chief Justice Lamer's wording, would not inhere in the very meaning of aboriginality.

For the SCC, the protection of Aboriginal cultural activities is only one way of accommodating Aboriginal peoples. Another means for pursuing accommodation is related to protecting particular Aboriginal territories. In the *Delgamuukw* case, Chief Justice Lamer argued that there is a significant connection between the lands claimed by Aboriginal peoples, their cultures, and aboriginality. After insisting that occupancy is a central consideration when settling a claim of Aboriginal title,[11] Chief Justice Lamer went on to state that

> occupancy is determined by reference to the activities that have taken place on the land and the uses to which the land has been put by the particular group. If lands are so occupied, there will exist a special bond between the group and the land in question such that the land will be part of the definition of the group's distinctive culture.[12]

Chief Justice Lamer put forward that territory plays a role in shaping a group's collective identity because it affects a group's culture. That is, the justification for Aboriginal title rests on identity-related and culture-related considerations.

Indeed, the connection between land and Aboriginal identity is so important for the court that it builds limits into the meaning of Aboriginal title in order to ensure that Aboriginal title lands continue to perform this culture-maintenance function. According to Chief Justice Lamer, "the content of aboriginal title contains an inherent limit that lands held pursuant to title cannot be used in a manner that is irreconcilable with the nature of the claimants' attachment to those lands."[13] The former chief justice argued that "the relevance of the continuity of the relationship of an aboriginal community with its land here is that it applies not only to the past, but to the future as well ... Uses of the lands that would threaten that future relationship are by their very nature excluded from the content of aboriginal title."[14] In this instance, the court outlined that only certain land uses would be a proper basis for Aboriginal title – uses that do not threaten or undermine the culture-maintenance function of traditional territories. As a result, Aboriginal cultures significantly impact the ways in which Aboriginal title lands can be used. For the court, the relationship between Aboriginal territories and cultures is one in which the former can be significantly limited by the latter.

By way of summary, there are a number of characteristics of section 35 rights that illustrate a concern for attachment to Aboriginal communities. For instance, section 35 rights protect practices, customs, and traditions that are integral and distinctive to the cultures of particular Aboriginal communities. That protection facilitates and, indeed, makes possible those kinds of attachments. Similarly, the section 35 framework offers the possibility of continuing, and even strengthening, attachments to Aboriginal communities by providing Aboriginal groups with the means to acquire title to traditional territories. Moreover, considerations centred on the pre-contact presence of Aboriginal communities are a constitutive part of the infringement-justification mechanism. Stated differently, these communities are of sufficient significance that they must be accounted for if the Crown is to make a legitimate case for infringing on a section 35 right. This is certainly significant in a legal system such as Canada's, where the sovereignty of parliament is a core principle. Thus, it is not an overstatement to say that attachments to Aboriginal communities are important aspects of the court's Aboriginal rights jurisprudence and its conception of aboriginality.

Attachment to the Pan-Canadian Community

A review of the SCC's rulings pertaining to Aboriginal rights cases illustrates that, for the justices, aboriginality entails a second constitutive element: attachment to the pan-Canadian political community. Membership in the pan-Canadian political community underpins the SCC's position that, at times, Aboriginal peoples ought to be treated in a manner akin to non-Aboriginal Canadians, regardless of their distinctiveness. For example, in the case of *Mitchell v. M.N.R.*, Justice Binnie explained that "the respondents and other aboriginal people live and contribute as part of our [non-Aboriginal Canadian] national diversity. So too in the court's definition of aboriginal rights."[15] Justice Binnie went on to add that "while an aboriginal person could be characterized as an Indian for some purposes including language, culture and the exercise of traditional rights, he or she does not cease thereby to be a resident of a province or territory. For other purposes he or she must be recognized and treated as an ordinary member of Canadian society."[16] Justice Binnie clearly expressed the view that, regardless of the existing differences between Aboriginal and non-Aboriginal Canadians, the former remain members of the pan-Canadian political community. And this is the justification for the claim that, under certain circumstances, Aboriginal peoples ought to be treated like any other members of that community.

In the case of *R. v. Gladstone,* the SCC made this exact point – that, at times, Aboriginal peoples ought to be treated in a manner akin to non-Aboriginals – and proposed that this type of treatment is justified even if it results in the infringement of Aboriginal rights. The SCC held the view that the infringement of section 35 rights is partially explained vis-à-vis the fact that Aboriginal peoples are simultaneously members of particular Aboriginal communities and the broader Canadian political community. Chief Justice Lamer states:

> Because, however, distinctive aboriginal societies exist within, and are a part of, a broader social, political and economic community, over which the Crown is sovereign, there are circumstances in which, in order to pursue objectives of compelling and substantial importance to that community as a whole (taking into account the fact that aboriginal societies are a part of that community), some limitation of those rights will be justifiable. Aboriginal rights are a necessary part of the reconciliation of aboriginal societies with the broader political community of which they are part; limits placed on those rights are, where the objectives furthered by those limits are of sufficient importance to the broader community as a whole, equally a necessary part of that reconciliation.[17]

For the SCC, the infringement of Aboriginal rights is not necessarily problematic because it can be an integral part of the process of reconciling Aboriginal and non-Aboriginal communities. More importantly, for our purposes here, the infringement of section 35 rights is explained vis-à-vis appeals to the fact that Aboriginal peoples are members of the pan-Canadian political community. In certain circumstances, Aboriginal rights may be infringed in order to pursue interests that are of importance to this broader community. And this is legitimate because Aboriginal peoples are also involved in this latter community. This is quite clear if one considers the SCC's list of legislative objectives that are capable of justifying the infringement of an Aboriginal right.[18] These objectives could be characterized as national concerns – that is, concerns that have the potential to impact multiple parts or even all of the pan-Canadian political community.[19]

Furthermore, the sovereignty of the Crown, which ostensibly represents all Canadians and so is about the pan-Canadian political community, plays an important role in section 35 jurisprudence. It is a factor in the process of justifying the infringement of an Aboriginal right. Specifically, if an Aboriginal right is not compatible with the sovereignty of the pan-Canadian political community, its infringement is justifiable. And concern for the pan-Canadian political community's sovereignty goes beyond the process for justifiably infringing Aboriginal rights. For example, it also plays a role at the identification stage of the test for Aboriginal rights as a temporal requirement. According to the framework for section 35, the significant historical moment is contact with Europeans (or, in the case of the Metis, the establishment of effective control by the Crown). This is the moment in which the Crown asserted or secured sovereignty. This temporal requirement works to ensure that, even at the stage where Aboriginal rights are identified, considerations that include the broader political community (in this case, in the form of the Crown's sovereignty) are factors in determining which practices, customs, and traditions are included in the section 35 constitutional provision.

The overall analysis outlined in this section is significant for two reasons. First, it demonstrates that part of the SCC's characterization of the collective identity of Aboriginal peoples includes the idea of membership in the pan-Canadian community, which under certain circumstances justifies treating Aboriginal peoples in a manner akin to other Canadians. Second, for the SCC, the fact of membership in the pan-Canadian community can limit the degree of protection afforded to Aboriginal peoples by section 35 rights. Indeed, at least for the SCC justices, the infringement of Aboriginal rights can be represented as a "good thing" when the limitation of rights facilitates the reconciliation of Aboriginal and non-Aboriginal communities.

Academic Commentary on Section 35 Rights

A number of prominent scholars engaged in the study of Aboriginal politics and the law have produced compelling critiques of the SCC's analytical framework for section 35. In what follows, I examine John J. Borrows's explanation of the rationale underlying the built-in limits of Aboriginal rights; Patrick Macklem's outline of the problems associated with Aboriginal title; and Justice Binnie's and Michael Asch's analyses of the absence of adequate self-governance rights in this framework. Even though these scholars focus their attention on different aspects of this constitutional provision and different Aboriginal rights cases, my examination demonstrates that a common thread binds their work. All of their critiques incorporate (to varying degrees and in various guises) the proposition that section 35 rights aim to protect the two constitutive elements of the citizen-state conceptualization of aboriginality – attachments to Aboriginal communities and to the pan-Canadian political community.

I begin with Borrows's work on *Sparrow*. He identifies the existence of a significant lacuna between what was claimed by the Aboriginal plaintiffs in the case and what was ultimately secured. According to Borrows, the Aboriginal plaintiffs in the *Sparrow* case were seeking significant powers of self-government. He states that "Aboriginal Peoples were claiming recognition of their ability to exercise regulatory authority in Canada in a manner similar, though with obvious differences, to that shared by the Dominion and provincial governments" (Borrows 2003, 233).[20] Borrows (2003, 233-34) points out that the SCC ignored that claim and instead offered a statement about the limits of section 35 by putting forward ways in which Aboriginal rights could be infringed by Canadian governments. He provides the following explanation for the SCC's motivations for doing so: "Placing limits on Aboriginal Rights presumably diminished fears that some people may have had that Aboriginal Rights could strain and potentially rip the fabric of federalism that had been operative to that point. Therefore one could speculate that the court held that Dominion laws could infringe Aboriginal Rights because of its concern for social cohesion" (Borrows 2003, 233-34). In Borrows's account, the motivation underpinning the SCC's focus on spelling out the limitations of section 35, instead of dealing with the jurisdictional issues raised by the Aboriginal plaintiffs, was a product of its concerns about the social cohesion of the entire pan-Canadian political community. The fact that concerns for the broader political community were cited as justifiable reasons for limiting the rights covered by the constitutional provision lends credence to the notion that section 35 rights are meant to protect the citizen-state conception of aboriginality. Aboriginal peoples under this conception are members of both an Aboriginal community and the pan-Canadian community, allowing the SCC to simultaneously advance that Aboriginal rights are capable of placing certain checks on the Crown's actions (in order to protect the Aboriginal community) and that those rights may be justifiably infringed (in order to protect the pan-Canadian community). Also of interest is that Borrows exposes how the expectations of the Aboriginal claimants in *Sparrow* were thwarted by the court's attempt to protect the citizen-state conception of aboriginality.

Macklem's explanation and critique of Aboriginal title parallel, in important ways, Borrows's account of the SCC's actions in *Sparrow*. Macklem (1997b, 134) advances that Aboriginal title, in some circumstances, provides a mechanism for Aboriginal nations to secure access to, use of, and even ownership over traditional territories. However, he goes on to argue that Aboriginal title has amounted to very little because it has failed to alter the Crown's proprietary power or legislative authority over the territories claimed by Aboriginal peoples (Macklem 1997b, 134). He also argues that this has created a situation wherein Aboriginal peoples are generally only able to enjoy title to lands that are of little interest to the Crown or third-party (and mostly non-Aboriginal) users (Macklem 1997b, 134). In short, section 35 provides a vehicle for Aboriginal peoples to secure title in some instances, but this vehicle is limited in serious ways. In instances where title is granted, the constitutional provision can be said to provide protection for Aboriginal peoples' attachments to their particular communities; in instances where title is denied, section 35 does not accomplish this. Of import are the reasons offered for the latter result. Macklem argues that the SCC justifies the latter case by citing concerns for ensuring the continued use and enjoyment of lands by the Crown and third-party users. These concerns can be framed as concerns about the broader pan-Canadian community.[21] It is evident that an important feature of Macklem's interpretation (and critique) of Aboriginal title is that it hinges on the court being concerned about Aboriginal peoples' attachments to specific Aboriginal communities and about the pan-Canadian community. This structure mirrors the citizen-state construction of aboriginality and lends credence to the argument that Aboriginal title under section 35 works to protect the constitutive elements of the citizen-state conception of the collective identity. In essence, the attempt to reconcile these concerns (concerns for the pan-Canadian political community and the Aboriginal communities) is a product of employing a citizen-state conception of aboriginality. That attempt is also the reason, according to Macklem, that Aboriginal title has failed to alter the proprietary power and legislative authority of the Crown – that is, the reason Aboriginal title has often failed to meet the needs and interests of Aboriginal peoples in Canada.

In his work on early section 35 jurisprudence, Justice Binnie takes the position that the SCC will be hesitant to read a broad right to self-government into this constitutional provision. The reasons Justice Binnie provides for his position echo those outlined by Borrows and Macklem. Specifically, he argues that concern for the pan-Canadian community will play a decisive role in shaping the decisions reached by the SCC in Aboriginal rights litigation. Justice Binnie (1990, 218) explains that

> the *Sparrow* doctrine makes it improbable that the judicial concept of Aboriginal right will extend to such key objectives as Aboriginal self-government. The application of the Supreme Court's interpretation of section 35 in *Sparrow* would afford too much immunity from other levels of government to Aboriginal communities, many of which lie cheek by jowl with non-Aboriginal communities ... "Constitutionalizing" a right to Aboriginal self-government would, in light of *Sparrow*, leave the courts with inadequate mechanisms to regulate the overlapping interests of communities occupying contiguous territory.

The limits of section 35, according to Justice Binnie, will be crafted with an eye to ensuring the stability of the broader pan-Canadian political community. In particular, he advances that the problems that could potentially result from multiple levels of government exercising overlapping and/or adjacent jurisdictional authority will ultimately make a judicially created right to Aboriginal self-government improbable. Concern for the pan-Canadian political community is part of Justice Binnie's views about the scope of section 35.

However, Justice Binnie's work on *Sparrow* also shows that section 35 is concerned with attachments to Aboriginal communities. Indeed, for Binnie (1990, 224), the SCC recognizes that Aboriginal Canadians' rights flow not only from membership in the pan-Canadian community – where "ordinary law," as he calls it, generates rights of universal citizenship – but rights also flow from membership in Aboriginal communities and nations. Thus, for Justice Binnie, section 35 takes into account the importance of particular Aboriginal communities (because they can generate collective rights) and the broader pan-Canadian political community (because it is viewed as the source of universal rights of citizenship). His is an account of section 35 that envisions protection of the two constitutive facets of a citizen-state conception of aboriginality.

I now turn to academic commentary on the sovereignty of the Crown, an important element of the issue of attachment to the pan-Canadian political community. According to Asch (1999, 437), since the *Van der Peet* decision, section 35 cannot include rights to self-determination or sovereignty, but rather rights that are best characterized as "way-of-life-rights." Asch (1999, 440) explains (correctly) that

> Aboriginal rights as constitutional rights are defined as the means by which the prior facts of Crown sovereignty and of the original occupation of the land by indigenous peoples are reconciled. Described in this manner, even if it included fundamental political rights, the concept of Aboriginal rights could never challenge Crown sovereignty, for, logically, a means to reconcile prior facts cannot also challenge the nature of those facts.

He concludes that "the judgment therefore implies that the courts will not acknowledge that Aboriginal peoples hold, or indeed ever held fundamental rights if such acknowledgment challenges the sovereignty of the Crown" (Asch 1999, 440). The central point to take away from Asch's critique of the *Van der Peet* decision is the following: Built into the very meaning of section 35 is the requirement that whatever rights are generated by the constitutional provision, they must be reconcilable with the sovereignty of the Crown. And concern for the sovereignty of the Crown is a key aspect of the second facet of the citizen-state conception of aboriginality. Consequently, one is able to make sense of the exclusion of important political rights that facilitate Aboriginal sovereignty and self-determination once one recognizes that the SCC's interpretation of section 35 aims at protecting the sovereignty of the Crown, a very important element of the citizen-state conception of aboriginality.

The commentaries on section 35 jurisprudence analyzed above include that the SCC's decision to protect the citizen-state version of aboriginality underpins what the court says about the limits of Aboriginal rights (Borrows's view), the limits of Aboriginal title (Macklem's work), and the limits of the rights of self-government (the views of Justice Binnie and Asch). And so, while these scholars make different claims and focus on different issues, they all illustrate the problems with anchoring Aboriginal rights to the reconciliation of attachments to Aboriginal communities and the pan-Canadian political community.

Conclusion

Attachment to a particular Aboriginal community represents one facet of the SCC's conception of aboriginality. The SCC's conception of aboriginality also entails that the attachments that Aboriginal peoples have with their communities must be balanced with their membership in the pan-Canadian political community and the Crown's sovereignty. Section 35 rights take the shape they do in order to protect these relations of attachment.

What comes to the fore in this chapter is the fact that, over the course of decades of section 35 litigation, even though the Aboriginal participants and some federal and provincial representatives offered two differing conceptions of aboriginality, the SCC did not adopt these conceptualizations. Just as it did in the early 1990s when it was confronted with competing positions regarding the aim of section 35 (i.e., the arguments that Aboriginal rights should be merely symbolic or should facilitate Aboriginal self-determination), the SCC went its own way. The court rejected the colonial and nation-to-nation conceptions of aboriginality and advanced a third conceptualization – the citizen-state version. And by the late 1990s/early 2000s, a number of attorneys general also advanced the SCC's conceptualization of aboriginality when they engaged in section 35 litigation. In the final two chapters of this book, I analyze the serious and unjust consequences for Aboriginal peoples of basing section 35 rights on the citizen-state understanding of aboriginality.

7

Aboriginal Rights Jurisprudence and Identity Contestation

As a result of the analysis in the previous two chapters, we can say that there are three distinct definitions of the term "aboriginality" in the Canadian Aboriginal rights jurisprudence – certainly an interesting empirical finding. However, since our primary concern is assessing the impact of identity contestation on rights (where the aim of rights is the protection of identity), our task is not yet complete. This is because the mere existence of different versions of a collective identity does not, in and of itself, automatically translate into a conflict over rights. After all, we can imagine a case where people hold different conceptualizations of a particular identity but do not disagree about the rights required to protect this identity. This could result from a number of factors, the most obvious being that the conceptualizations in question share enough common ground that they are all adequately protected by the same set of rights. If we apply this logic to the analysis pursued here, we realize that in order for us to be able to say that the identity dispute is connected to the rights dispute, we need to not only illustrate that the parties involved in section 35 litigation put forward different understandings of aboriginality, but that the rights outlined by the Supreme Court of Canada (SCC) fail to protect the versions of aboriginality held by the parties to the cases. Doing so would illustrate that the lack of consensus over the meaning of aboriginality in the legal material is, indeed, a potential source of the rights conflict. That is, the parties' different versions of aboriginality could be a reason for their different ideas about the scope of Aboriginal rights, because different rights would be required in order to protect the understanding of the collective identity held by each party.

In this chapter, I outline the argument for this last claim. Specifically, I examine the degree to which section 35 rights can, in principle, protect the colonial and nation-to-nation conceptions of aboriginality. The examination demonstrates that Aboriginal rights in their current form cannot protect these two conceptions. And, while it is my position that we should not be concerned about a lack of protection for the colonial conception of aboriginality, we certainly have cause to be concerned about a lack of protection for the nation-to-nation conception of this collective identity. The case for my position on the colonial conception is outlined in this chapter, while the case for my position on the nation-to-nation conception is presented in the next chapter.

One may wonder why I do not include the citizen-state conception in the analysis. The reason is that my analysis of the legal material thus far supports the argument that the citizen-state conception of aboriginality is, in principle, compatible with section 35. Insofar as my reading of the legal material is correct, I advance that the SCC has constructed section 35 rights so as to protect the citizen-state version of aboriginality in order to accommodate Aboriginal peoples.

Furthermore, given that section 35 rights are constructed so as to protect the citizen-state conception of the Aboriginal collective identity, I assert that any failure to protect this conception of aboriginality is a failure of application. This allows for the possibility that section 35 rights do not always end up protecting the citizen-state conception of aboriginality. For example, it is possible that, from time to time, judges make mistakes and rule in ways that end up undermining, as opposed to protecting, the citizen-state version of aboriginality. The point I advance is not about the results of specific interpretations of section 35, but about compatibility at the conceptual level. I base this on the assumption that the justices of the SCC would not outline a set of rights that is, in principle, incapable of protecting their understanding of aboriginality, because doing so would be irrational. As a result, we need not concern ourselves with the citizen-state conception of aboriginality.

Section 35 Rights and the Colonial Conception

In order to ascertain if section 35 rights can protect a particular conception of aboriginality, we must determine the degree to which these rights are compatible with the conception's constitutive elements. Accordingly, when the colonial conception is the subject of analysis, we need to figure out if and how these rights protect the external (i.e., non-Aboriginal) definition of aboriginality and the external rule of Aboriginal peoples.

There are a number of elements of the SCC's Aboriginal rights jurisprudence that indicate that external definition of aboriginality is not wholly compatible with section 35 rights. For instance, consider the first two steps involved in pursing an Aboriginal rights claim – identifying a specific Aboriginal right and demonstrating its prima facie infringement. According to the court, the Aboriginal claimant is charged with defining the specific nature and content of the Aboriginal right that is the subject of the section 35 claim. Given that Aboriginal rights aim to protect aboriginality, this will inevitably entail the Aboriginal claimant presenting a characterization of the collective identity (see Chapter 2). Stated somewhat differently, in order to make the case that Aboriginal group X has a section 35 right to Y, the group will have to illustrate that Y is necessary for the protection of the group's understanding of its collective identity. And there are numerous examples of the court accepting an Aboriginal group's characterization of its particular collective identity, as well as its arguments regarding the necessity of a specific Aboriginal right.

Of course, this does not mean that Aboriginal claimants' characterizations of aboriginality will always be accepted by the court. Nor does this mean that the court will always accept Aboriginal claimants' arguments regarding the necessity of a particular right. These matters are determined over the course of litigation. What is of import, for our purposes, is that Aboriginal claimants do, in fact, have the opportunity to present their conception of aboriginality when engaged in Aboriginal rights litigation. Thus, it is incorrect to say that when the meaning of aboriginality is at issue during section 35 litigation, it is exclusively the product of external definition. And this indicates that section 35 rights are not compatible with a conception of aboriginality that requires that the collective identity be defined by outsiders – such as the colonial conception.

What about the second important facet of the colonial version of aboriginality? Do section 35 rights allow for external (i.e., non-Aboriginal) rule of Aboriginal peoples? The jurisprudence provides a somewhat mixed response. On the one hand, certain statements by the justices of the SCC about the sovereignty of the Crown certainly lend credence to the idea that Aboriginal rights are compatible with (and, indeed facilitate) the external rule of Aboriginal peoples. The court's comments regarding the Crown's sovereignty in the *Sparrow* case are often cited to illustrate this point. The court stated that "there was from the outset never any doubt that sovereignty and legislative power, and indeed the underlying title, to such lands vested in the Crown."[1] In this early section 35 case, the court made a clear and unambiguous pronouncement about its position regarding the legitimacy of the Crown's political authority over Aboriginal peoples and territories.[2] Consequently, there is evidence for the notion that section 35 rights support the external rule of Aboriginal peoples.

On the other hand, over the course of more than twenty years of section 35 jurisprudence, the court has never explicitly stated that Aboriginal peoples do not have a section 35 right to self-government. Interestingly, in the *Pamajewon* case, the court went out of its way to say that it was *not* ruling on whether such a right exists. The court even provided some guidelines for properly framing a claim for this type of right. In my view, the fact that the SCC has never denied the existence of a section 35 right to self-government and its willingness to speculate on the proper way for Aboriginal peoples to frame this kind of rights claim are two good reasons for believing that, given the right circumstance, the SCC would support some sort of a section 35 right to self-government.

Furthermore, some scholars have advanced that at least since the *Haida Nation* and *Taku River* decisions, the court seems to be "softening" the way it talks about the sovereignty of the Crown. For example, Brian Slattery (2005, 437–38) puts forward that the court has gone from talking about the Crown's "acquisition" of sovereignty to talking about the Crown's "assertion" of sovereignty. The change in terminology is important because the first seems to provide a justification for the Crown's sovereignty (because acquisition generally implies some sort of legitimate exchange or transfer), while the second does not. After all, to assert something entails putting it out there without any (or sufficient) justification. According to Slattery (2005, 437–38), the change in language has allowed the court to discuss how the Crown's sovereignty is in tension with the original sovereignty held by Aboriginal nations. Together, the court's position on a section 35 right to self-government and its evolving discourse on the sovereignty of the Crown indicate that the court does not support a notion of external rule of Aboriginal peoples that is *exclusive* in nature. That is, while the SCC may not be forcing open the door to Aboriginal self-government, it is certainly not permanently barring the door shut

In summary, section 35 fails to facilitate external definition because it provides Aboriginal peoples with the opportunity to present their understanding of aboriginality, and this Aboriginal understanding has been the basis for specific section 35 rights. Moreover, while section 35 does not preclude the external rule of Aboriginal peoples, it also does not preclude Aboriginal self-government. As a consequence, the SCC's Aboriginal rights jurisprudence does not offer much by way of protection for the colonial conception of aboriginality.

In my view, we should applaud this result. Under this conception of aboriginality, being Aboriginal basically means non-Aboriginals tell Aboriginal peoples who they are and how they should live. And this is morally troubling. Aboriginal peoples themselves contest the moral rightness of external definitions of aboriginality (Mercredi and Turpel 1993, 24–25). Along the same lines, many compelling philosophical accounts advance that nations have a moral claim to self-determination, at least of some sort (e.g., Miller 1995, 81; Moore 1997). And that claim to self-determination has been recognized in international law.[3] In short, treating people in the way envisioned by the colonial conception is certainly morally problematic. And if that treatment is wrong, offering up rights to facilitate that treatment must be wrong as well. As far as the colonial version of aboriginality is concerned, the faster it is consigned to the dustbin of history, the better.

The above analysis is also useful because it highlights an important point: that the colonial conception of aboriginality is different from the citizen-state conception. The set of rights that is capable of protecting one conception is not capable of protecting the other. Specifically, different rights are required in order to protect a conception of aboriginality that is premised on external definition and external rule, versus a conception of aboriginality that is premised on balancing attachments to Aboriginal and pan-Canadian communities. In my view, keeping this difference in mind is an asset if one aims to provide a robust critique of the ways of conceptualizing aboriginality. In Chapter 8, I make the case that the citizen-state conception of aboriginality is also a problematic basis for section 35 rights, and the court's decision to use this version of the collective identity results in misrecognition and unfairness – two significant instances of harm. My main point is that, even though both the colonial and citizen-state conceptions of aboriginality are problematic, they are problematic for different reasons.

Section 35 Rights and the Nation-to-Nation Conception

Self-definition and self-government play a primary role in the nation-to-nation version of aboriginality put forward by Aboriginal participants in section 35 cases (see Chapter 6). The question of interest for us is the degree to which section 35 rights protect these two central components of the nation-to-nation version of aboriginality. In order to address this question, I turn to the scholarly literature on section 35. While each of the scholars included in the following assessment focuses on different aspects of section 35 rights, taken together, their work illustrates that these rights limit or erode Aboriginal nations' capacities to engage in self-definition and self-government. On this basis, I advance that Aboriginal rights in their current state cannot protect a nation-to-nation understanding of aboriginality.

Lee Maracle's critique of section 35 centres on the justices' mischaracterization of aboriginality and its impact on Aboriginal self-definition. For Maracle (2003, 312), the court's understanding of aboriginality is based on a conception of the collective identity that is the product of nineteenth-century non-Aboriginal anthropological "expertise." Maracle insists that what Aboriginal peoples require (and so, should have been provided by the court) are the tools (political, legal, and economic) to challenge this mischaracterization of aboriginality and to expose its complicity in creating and maintaining colonial relations between Aboriginal and non-Aboriginal populations. Maracle (2003, 312) concludes that this result would have been a far more useful course than engaging in a debate about the nature of aboriginality where the parameters are spelled out solely by non-Aboriginal "experts." What is of import for us is that this scholar's critique of section 35 is based on concerns about self-definition. Her critique sheds serious doubt on the idea that section 35 can protect this aspect of the nation-to-nation conception of aboriginality.

Aboriginal self-definition is also an important consideration in legal scholar Kent McNeil's critical analysis of Aboriginal title. For him, Aboriginal title is problematic because of the limits placed on Aboriginal self-definition. McNeil (1998, 9) begins his analysis by pointing out that the SCC's construction of Aboriginal title has a built-in limitation – namely, that any patterns of use that would prevent future Aboriginal generations from using ancestral territories in certain historically relevant ways are not candidates for section 35 protection. So, for example, certain economic activities based on resource extraction (such as mining) on Aboriginal title lands would not be allowed if they were to render impossible the activities (e.g., hunting, trapping, fishing, and the like) cited as the basis for claiming this title in the first place. This is a substantial limit of Aboriginal title.[4]

This built-in limitation underpins McNeil's (1998, 10) argument that Aboriginal title renders Aboriginal peoples "prisoners of the past" since, as he explains, "present uses are not restricted to, but they are restricted by, past practices and traditions." The problem, he explains, is that given the connection between Aboriginal lands and Aboriginal cultures and societies, court-defined and court-imposed limits on Aboriginal title translate into court-defined and court-imposed limits on aboriginality. McNeil (1998, 10) asks, "what if an Aboriginal society has changed so that its members no longer use their lands as they once did – they now have a different relationship with the land, which is still special to them, but is not historically based?" The current construction of Aboriginal title would offer little protection for relationships to land that fall into this category. And as a consequence, Aboriginal title would not provide any protection for the Aboriginal cultures, societies, and collective identities that are shaped by such relations. If Aboriginal title acts to protect certain relationships that Aboriginal peoples have with their claimed territories and if, in certain instances, they are not the relationships that are of significance for the maintenance of Aboriginal culture, society, and identity, then, from the perspective of the holders of section 35 rights, the efficacy of the section 35 right to protect their collective identity is quite dubious. McNeil (1998, 12) sums up his criticism by advancing that "Canadian courts should not sit in judgment over social change in Aboriginal communities, deciding what is and what is not necessary for their cultural preservation."

His criticism goes beyond the results of including the aforementioned limitations into the meaning of Aboriginal title. It extends to encompass the role that the SCC has assigned itself as a result of placing these limits on section 35 territorial rights. McNeil (1998, 12–13) concludes that "any internal limitations on Aboriginal title in the interests of cultural preservation should be determined by Aboriginal nations through the exercise of self-government within their communities – they should not be imposed by Canadian courts." Doing otherwise, he argues, is simply an exercise in paternalism (McNeil 1998, 11).

McNeil's dissatisfaction with the SCC's construction of Aboriginal title is related to his concerns about self-definition in two important ways. First, McNeil is critical of the kinds of relationships to the land that the SCC has described as worthy of constitutional protection, because he believes that they are not necessarily the ones that the holders of section 35 rights would or do select. Second, McNeil is critical of the fact that the court has assigned itself a role in guiding the evolutionary development of aboriginality by determining which relationships are worthy of section 35 protection. In other words, he is critical of the way in which the SCC has taken on the task of defining what aboriginality is and which parts of it will be protected. His assessment of the current construction of Aboriginal title exposes how Aboriginal peoples' ability to define their own collective identities is limited – by not allowing them to select the relationships with the land that *they* see as important for the maintenance of their cultures and societies.

Ronald Niezen's work reveals a similar concern regarding the manner in which the SCC's interpretation of section 35 hampers Aboriginal peoples' ability to define themselves (both in the present and in the future). He focuses his criticism on the SCC's test for identifying Aboriginal rights. According to Niezen (2003a, 9), the SCC focuses too much attention on historical cultural practices, customs, and traditions, to the detriment of cultural change and innovation.[5]

The first problem with such an approach, Niezen argues, is that it presents a version of aboriginality that is overly determined by the past. The second problem is that it results in rights that not only are anchored to a specific historical moment, but that cannot protect societal or cultural changes that aim to secure the survival of members of the collective group. Niezen (2003a, 7) states that innovations that took place after the arrival of settlers are not seen as being integral to tradition. A "frozen in time" approach to culture is thus avoided only in the sense that practices can survive some discontinuity, not in a sense that affirms the importance of adaptation, creativity and innovation. The judicial approach to culture is thus "frozen in time" in the truest sense of the term: it sets limits on change, even in response to challenges to the prosperity and survival of distinct cultures as a whole.

From this view, section 35 rights encompass practices, traditions, and customs of a historical nature to a far greater degree than they do societal and cultural changes, innovations, and adaptations developed by Aboriginal peoples in their efforts to survive as distinctive communities and nations. Niezen argues that adaptation, creativity, and innovation – elements that are of significance to the process of self-definition – are at odds with this constitutional provision. This appears to be so even when adaptation, creativity, and innovation are employed by Aboriginal peoples in their efforts to secure their cultural and societal survival. The current interpretation of section 35 is very much anathema to these aspects of self-definition, and so to the nation-to-nation version of aboriginality.

The notion that section 35 leaves little room for self-definition is echoed by other scholars. Commenting on the *Pamajewon* decision, legal scholar Bradford W. Morse (1997, 1031) characterizes the SCC's approach as a "judicial assessment of historical, sociological and anthropological evidence of what constitutes a culture that was freeze-dried at the time of contact with Europeans." He argues that "such an approach tells Aboriginal peoples that what is relevant about them is their past – not their present or future" (Morse 1997, 1031). He concludes by insisting that this approach "excludes what may have become, or what may become in the future, integral to the survival of Aboriginal cultures" (Morse 1997, 1032). The basic proposition underlying Morse's critique of section 35 is that the SCC based the constitutional provision on its own version of aboriginality, which is unable to account for certain kinds of change (even when change may be an important factor in the maintenance of the Aboriginal collective identity). In this instance, not only is there a mischaracterization of aboriginality, but the mischaracterization takes the place of Aboriginal self-definition. Morse's analysis (as well as Maracle's and McNeil's) is distressing because it demonstrates how the SCC's conception of aboriginality sets significant limits on what is and what is not the proper subject of constitutional protection. Furthermore, the SCC's conception of aboriginality creates a situation wherein those who ultimately shoulder the costs of getting it wrong (i.e., constructing section 35 rights that fail to adequately protect the Aboriginal collective identity) are the bearers of the collective identity who, as it turns out, did not participate in the setting of those limits in the first place.

Does the current interpretation of section 35 provide rights that protect self-government, the second constitutive feature of the nation-to-nation understanding of aboriginality? Many scholars explain that we have good reasons to be skeptical. According to Jennifer E. Dalton (2006, 19), the SCC "effectively restricted the scope of Aboriginal rights under section 35(1), most notably the right of Aboriginal self-government." Michael Murphy (2001a, 121) characterizes the existing legal framework for section 35 as a "potentially fatal blow to the hopes for any future recognition of a broad and liberal right of Aboriginal self-government."

There are two basic problems with the framework for section 35 developed by the court. First, the rights that come out of this framework must be specific and concrete. For example, in the *Gladstone* case, the right at issue was characterized as the right to harvest herring spawn on kelp, as opposed to a more general formulation such as an Aboriginal right to a coastal fishery. It is difficult to characterize self-government rights in such a narrow fashion. These rights are best described in a broad and somewhat general way. For example, Murphy (2001a, 109) puts forward that Aboriginal self-government (like self-government exercised by any nation) entails such things as "the right to decide on forms of land ownership and tenure, to make economic and social policy, to design legal and political institutions, and to preserve and promote a distinctive language and culture." Thus, Christie (2007, 19) is right to argue that

> self-government rights are not like other Aboriginal rights (as these have been defined by Canadian courts, as with, for example, hunting and fishing rights). While a right to engage in some sort of physical activity may make some minimal sense within the sort of framework established in *Sparrow*, *Delgamuukw*, and *Van der Peet*, governance rights are simply not amenable to being viewed as a right to engage in

physical activities, and treated as if each sub-right could represent a "custom" or "tradition."

The second problem with the legal framework for section 35 relates to what the SCC says about the sovereignty of the Crown. And Christie's work is instructive here as well. In his critique of the SCC's jurisprudence, Christie (2007, 11) explains that the doctrine of sovereign incompatibility (the proposition that an Aboriginal right cannot be incompatible with the sovereignty of the Crown) permanently robs Aboriginal nations of anything approaching the types of powers we would usually associate with self-government. Under the existing legal framework for section 35, the best that Aboriginal nations can hope for are powers that "would be 'internal', limited to matters that were directly related to (a) what remained of their lands, and to (b) their own people" (Christie 2007, 11–12). This is far from the type of self-government envisioned by Aboriginal peoples (see, for example, how Aboriginal self-government is characterized by Aboriginal peoples during section 35 litigation in Chapter 6). And this leads Christie (2007, 20) to conclude, rightly, that, "if self-government rights are simply treated like other Aboriginal rights under *Van der Peet*, they will not be self-government rights."

The analysis illustrates that the interpretation of section 35 offered by the SCC does not protect Aboriginal processes of self-definition or self-government. The scholars canvassed in this section are critical of section 35 rights, in part and indirectly, because they cannot protect the version of aboriginality put forward by the bearers of the collective identity. In their own way, all of these scholars take issue with the way in which the SCC characterizes aboriginality. All of their concerns speak to the incompatibility of section 35 rights and the nation-to-nation version of aboriginality.

Conclusion

Confronted with competing conceptions of aboriginality over the course of section 35 litigation, the SCC handled the identity dispute by rejecting the nation-to-nation and colonial versions of aboriginality. In their stead, the SCC based Aboriginal rights on the citizen-state conception of aboriginality – an understanding of the collective identity first introduced by the court. In this chapter, what becomes clear is that that decision impacts those who hold alternative views of aboriginality, because section 35 rights cannot protect their conceptions of the collective identity. And as a result, we have sufficient grounds for putting forward that part of the controversy surrounding section 35 is rightly characterized as a dispute about the meaning of aboriginality.

More importantly, while there may be good reason to celebrate the fact that section 35 rights do not protect the colonial conception of aboriginality, we certainly have sufficient cause to wonder about the impact of establishing a set of rights that is incapable of protecting the version of the collective identity put forward by those who are members of the identity group. In Chapter 8, I outline and assess the consequences of the court's decision to link section 35 rights to the citizen-state conception.

8

A Problematic Conception of Rights

Some may remark that choosing one conception of aboriginality, as the justices of the Supreme Court of Canada (SCC) did, is not all that surprising given the degree of irreconcilability between the different articulations of aboriginality. Others may add that extending protection to only one conception of aboriginality is not blameworthy behaviour – after all, it may have been inevitable, a constitutive element of the task that was before the SCC. Indeed, Indigenous studies professor Peter Kulchyski (1994, 2) explains that some scholars wrongly take the position that "it is the job of the courts to take on the role of defining, fixing and circumscribing Aboriginal rights." I challenge the notion that the SCC pursued the right course of action when it linked Aboriginal rights to the citizen-state conception of aboriginality. I do so by highlighting two problems with this decision; one is primarily about process and the other is about consequences. First, the justices of the SCC failed to outline their reasons for linking section 35 rights to the citizen-state conception of aboriginality, and so, a part of the jurisprudence on section 35 suffers from a serious justificatory gap. Second, section 35 not only fails to protect the nation-to-nation conception of aboriginality, but it also results in harm to Aboriginal peoples that manifests as misrecognition and unfairness.

The Jurisprudential Justification Gap

When we talk about justification, we generally refer to the provision of certain types of reasons. As T.M. Scanlon (2002, 140) explains, "to claim that a *principle* or *judgement* is justified is to say that it is supported by good or sufficient reasons." So, justification refers to providing reasons that are good enough for a reasonable person to believe that a proposition is true or right or good or some such similar thing.

Moreover, the act of justification is a particular type of activity. For philosopher A. John Simmons (1999, 740), justification is best thought of as a "defensive concept"; accordingly, he correctly claims that "we ask for justification against the background presumption of possible objection." What Simmons draws to our attention is that (all things being equal) one is not required to engage in the justification of that which is deemed to be (at least on the face of it) unobjectionable. So, for example, we generally do not require one to justify claims of the following sort: "Slavery is immoral" or "The innocent should not be made to pay for the crimes of the guilty."

However, when citizens are engaged in litigation with one another or with the state, we should assume the type of background objection described by Simmons. We require judges to provide us with (good) reasons for their decisions. We want justifications in order to make sure that judges did not act "wrongly" – that they did not make a mistake in applying and interpreting the law or misuse their power. Concerns about judges basing decisions on personal bias (as opposed to the law) represent one of most serious instances of the misuse of judicial power. By bias, I have in mind what philosopher Robert Nozick (1993, 6) explains as "personal preferences or prejudices, moods of the moment, partiality for one side in the dispute, or even thought-through moral and political principles that are personal." He argues that "a judge's own views, preferences, or even considered views should have no more effect than anybody else's – the judge was not given the institutional position to put her own preferences into effect" (Nozick 1993, 6). Thus, scholars of the Canadian judiciary are right to advance that written reasons are essential for maintaining citizens' confidence in the judiciary (Macfarlane 2013, 101). The SCC itself has offered similar commentary on the importance of written reasons and how these are linked to judicial accountability.[1]

Aside from the issues of institutional confidence and accountability, I believe that it is safe to say that as citizens, we feel as though we are entitled to judicial justifications. And according to legal scholar Mark Elliott, we are right to feel this way. He argues that it is not enough for agents of the state (judges included) to tell citizens that things have not gone their way; they need to tell them why. This is part of what it means to treat citizens with dignity (Elliott 2012, 62–63). What is at issue for us is whether the SCC decision to base section 35 on the citizen-state version of aboriginality is justified – where we understand justification to involve the provision of good or sufficient reasons.

No one can say that the SCC does not justify its section 35 jurisprudence in a general sense. After all, the justices provide written reasons for all of their section 35 rulings. Indeed, many of their written judgments are both extensive and lengthy. The *Delgamuukw* decision, for example, is a staggering 131 pages. The issue for us, however, is not whether the SCC provides justifications in a general sense, but if it provides an adequate justification for one specific (though important) part of its section 35 jurisprudence – that is, whether it explains why it decided to base section 35 rights on the citizen-state version of aboriginality.

The fact is that the SCC does not at any point provide such a justification. This is a serious shortcoming, since collective identity plays such a big part in setting out the scope of section 35 rights. Furthermore, the court's silence as to why it did not select the nation-to-nation version of aboriginality (even though it is the understanding of aboriginality consistently put forward by the Aboriginal participants) can be considered an act of disrespect. As Elliott (2012) explains, justification is needed in order to treat people with dignity; thus, failing to outline why the Aboriginal peoples' position was rejected on such an important issue is a failure to treat the Aboriginal participants with the appropriate level of dignity.

Some may point out, quite rightly, that section 35 rights as currently constructed sometimes do result in the protection of Aboriginal peoples' collective identities. There is no reason why, for example, certain identity-based interests of particular Aboriginal populations that are compatible with the citizen-state conception of aboriginality could not receive a degree of protection from the exercise of these group rights. The thing to keep in mind here, however, is that the protection that would occur would always be contingent on this aforementioned compatibility. As a consequence, in instances where Aboriginal peoples' identity-based interests contradict the citizen-state conception, no protection can result from the exercise of section 35 rights.

This result is connected to the issue of justification in an important way. Recall that according to the SCC, the purpose of section 35 is to accommodate Aboriginal peoples by protecting their collective identities (Chapter 1). We have seen that correspondence (i.e., holding a version of aboriginality that is compatible with the one held by the justices of the SCC) is a condition of accommodation. A significant problem immediately follows from approaching accommodation in this fashion. It is difficult to imagine that demanding this kind of correspondence as a condition for accommodation could meet a reasonable standard of fairness. As political theorist Joseph Carens (2003, 11) argues, "it is not fair to make people conform to a culture and an identity that they have not accepted themselves, or to marginalize them if they do not, at least when possible."[2] Carens puts forward that problems of fairness can result from demanding that members of a group embrace a collective identity (or version of a collective identity) that does not correspond with their own understanding. Moreover, he argues that demanding correspondence as a condition of accommodation should only be pursued in rare circumstances, when an alternative course of action is not available.

If this line of reasoning is applied to the case at hand, the SCC's decision to base section 35 on a citizen-state conception of aboriginality (and thus, to require correspondence as a condition of accommodation) can only be justified if alternatives are unavailable. By way of example, the SCC would have to show that basing section 35 rights on a nation-to-nation conception is somehow unworkable, even though there are examples of what such an interpretation of section 35 would look like (e.g., Canada 1996; Borrows 2010). The SCC, however, failed to provide this type of justification because it did not provide reasons for its use of the citizen-state version of aboriginality. It simply asserted this understanding of aboriginality as if it were an uncontested or (perhaps more disturbingly) an uncontestable empirical reality. And as the analysis of the court material showed by the presence of competing definitions of aboriginality, this was not the case.

Thus, the SCC's interpretation of section 35 creates a justificatory gap that leaves unaddressed both the reasons why the citizen-state version of the collective identity is the proper object of constitutional protection and the reasons why demanding correspondence as a condition of accommodation is a legitimate requirement for the exercise of section 35 rights. We have no way of deciding whether there were good or sufficient reasons for this course of action. Without these reasons, the SCC's section 35 jurisprudence fails to meet an acceptable standard of justification on these important matters.

Harming Aboriginal Peoples: Misrecognition and Unfairness

The decision to link section 35 to the citizen-state conception of aboriginality has another set of serious consequences. The consequences are so serious, in fact, that it is right to talk about them as instances of harm. By harm, I mean damage to an individual or to interests that are vitally important to an individual. In what follows, I outline how the decision to connect section 35 rights to the citizen-state conception results in harm in two ways: first, harm results from the misrecognition of Aboriginal peoples, and second, it results from treating Aboriginal peoples unfairly.

Political philosopher Charles Taylor (1994, 25), in his work on the politics of recognition, explains that

> our identity is partly shaped by recognition or its absence, often by the misrecognition of others, and so a person or group of people can suffer real damage, real distortion, if the people or society around them mirror back to them a confining or demeaning or contemptible picture of themselves. Nonrecognition or misrecognition can inflict harm, can be a form of oppression, imprisoning someone in a false, distorted, and reduced mode of being.

The basic point is that misrecognition can result in real and serious harm to individuals. Taylor (1994, 64) underscores the seriousness of this harm by equating it with the harm that arises from forms of injustice such as inequality and exploitation. In the case of section 35, misrecognition is a result of the (unjustified) rejection of the Aboriginal participants' nation-to-nation version of aboriginality and the decision to tie section 35 rights to the citizen-state conception. From the point of view of Aboriginal peoples, the SCC has misrecognized them. And, even more seriously, section 35 constitutionalizes this misrecognition. They are (to use Taylor's phraseology) prisoners of the citizen-state conception of aboriginality.

It is true that some scholars find Taylor's work on the "politics of recognition" an inappropriate analytical lens when the topic of concern is the relationship between Aboriginal peoples and the state. Glen Coulthard's work is a good example of this position. Coulthard (2007, 442–43) argues that "where 'recognition' is conceived as something that is 'granted' ... or 'accorded' ... to a subaltern group or entity [it fails] to significantly modify, let alone transcend, the breadth of power at play in colonial relationships." For Coulthard, the inherent logic of the concept of recognition makes it unable to do the analytical and prescriptive work that Taylor describes.

I do not dispute that the discourse of the politics of recognition may, indeed, suffer from the problems identified by scholars such as Coulthard. Coulthard's critique of this discourse, however, does not negate the claim that misrecognition is harmful, or even that it is harmful in the way outlined by Taylor. We still have good reason to accept Taylor's characterization of the problem of misrecognition (and the resulting harms), even if we are convinced by Coulthard that Taylor's analysis suffers from certain limitations and that his proposed solutions are inadequate. In short, we can continue to hold the view that the decision to anchor section 35 rights to the citizen-state conception of aboriginality is an instance of misrecognition of Aboriginal peoples, and so it is harmful.

Unfairness is the other instance of harm that results from the court's decision to tie section 35 rights to the citizens-state conception of aboriginality. By unfairness, I mean something more substantive than what the term can sometimes entail in common parlance – that is, a simple inequity of some kind (e.g., when I say that it is unfair that you received a bigger piece of cake than I). I use the term "unfairness" in the way that it is often used in philosophy – that is, to convey the idea of treatment that is not compatible with justice. And so, to treat someone unfairly is to do them an injustice and thus to harm them.

In their work on section 35, Halie Bruce and Ardith Walkem put forward that this constitutional provision entails a particular kind of uneven exchange between Aboriginal peoples and the Canadian state. They argue that,

> in order for Indigenous Peoples to achieve any protection under s.35(1), all of the following are recognized and protected first: (1) Canadian sovereignty and nationhood; (2) Canadian Crown title to all of our [Aboriginal] territories; and (3) Canadian governments' rights to make laws about our territories and resources. In exchange for recognizing

Crown sovereignty, title and jurisdiction, Indigenous Peoples are entitled to Aboriginal Rights. (Bruce and Walkem 2003, 350)

Bruce and Walkem advance that protecting the citizen-state version of aboriginality comes at a very high price: Aboriginal acceptance of the legitimacy of the Crown's claims to sovereignty and to jurisdiction over Aboriginal territories. And this is problematic for a number of reasons.

First, with regard to the Crown's sovereignty, Brian Slattery (2005, 435) advances that some Aboriginal peoples "deny outright that the Crown ever gained lawful sovereignty over them, arguing that they were never conquered by the Crown and never voluntarily ceded their territories to the Crown or accepted its claims of authority." He concludes that "in one way or another, then, Crown sovereignty has always been a sticking point for Aboriginal peoples" (Slattery 2005, 435). And yet, if Bruce and Walkem are correct, Aboriginal peoples who decide to use Aboriginal rights (in their current form) are forced to accept (at least tacitly) the sovereignty of the Crown. In my view, Bruce and Walkem are right about this implication. Since Aboriginal rights are based on an understanding of aboriginality that includes an important role for the sovereignty of the Crown, then the decision to use those rights can be understood to entail the implied acceptance of that component of the rights. Given Slattery's position regarding Aboriginal views about the sovereignty of the Crown, this is certainly a dilemma. And given the judicial justification gap and the harm that results from misrecognition, it is difficult to imagine that putting Aboriginal peoples in such a situation meets any reasonable standard of fairness.

The problem, however, is more serious than simply having to hold one's nose when using Aboriginal rights. For many scholars, the Crown's sovereignty and title are the very mechanisms that have led to Aboriginal peoples' dispossession, displacement, and disappearance (Tully 2000a, 39–40; Chartrand 2003, 462; Walkem 2003). As D'Arcy Vermette (2011, 72) so forcefully concludes in his work on section 35, "the process and practice of colonialism necessarily involves the confiscation, theft, dispossession of Aboriginal peoples' lands, lives, and culture. This is not a mere inconvenience for Aboriginal peoples. Simply put, the law is contributing to the destruction of entire peoples." This is the reason why these mechanisms need to be challenged and changed. Indeed, Tully (2000a, 38) argues that, at least since the mid-nineteenth century, what is referred to as "Aboriginal resistance" is characterized by attempts to challenge and change these very mechanisms.

The basic point is that the Crown's sovereignty and title are instruments that have harmed and continue to harm Aboriginal individuals and their communities. This fact makes it unfair to ask Aboriginal peoples to accept a set of rights that protects a version of their collective identity that they do not hold and that comes at the cost of leaving the principal tools of Aboriginal subordination undisturbed. Bruce and Walkem (2003, 356–57) sum up this position aptly, arguing that "S.35 rights – defined so as not to upset any existing political order or interests of Canada – are not tools of our survival, but markers of our colonized status."

Uncoupling Section 35 Rights from the Citizen-State Conception

One may wonder how the analysis of section 35 would differ if the constitutional provision were connected to a conception of aboriginality other than the citizen-state conception. Would the various problems plaguing the current form of Aboriginal rights in Canada be avoided? The answer to this question would inevitably involve speculation, but I offer the following thoughts. I have already explained how the colonial conception is morally problematic (see Chapter 7). In my view, that fact alone should suffice to disqualify it as an acceptable basis for Aboriginal rights. Thus, I add only two additional points. Given that the colonial conception of aboriginality (a version premised on external definition and external rule) is the polar opposite of the nation-to-nation conception (a version premised on self-definition and self-government), constitutionalizing that version of aboriginality would still constitute a serious act of misrecognition. Indeed, it would constitute a much more serious act of misrecognition. A colonial version of aboriginality would also leave the principal mechanisms of Aboriginal subordination (i.e., the Crown's sovereignty and title) untouched, and so Aboriginal peoples would continue to be treated unfairly. Since both of these results would continue the harm currently done by section 35, the colonial conception of aboriginality does not represent any sort of improvement.

On the other hand, employing a nation-to-nation understanding of aboriginality would produce a different outcome. It would avoid the problems that result from the misrecognition of Aboriginal peoples, because the object of constitutional protection would be the version of aboriginality advanced by Aboriginal peoples themselves. That would be a positive development in the sense that any harm that currently results from misrecognition would be eliminated. Moreover, the justificatory gap, which marks the existing jurisprudence on Aboriginal rights, would disappear. It would disappear because the justices would no longer be required to explain to the claimants of Aboriginal rights why things did not go their way. Thus, there is some basis for advancing that an Aboriginal rights provision premised on the nation-to-nation understanding of aboriginality would represent an improvement on the current situation.

My intention is not to claim that section 35 rights premised on a nation-to-nation conception of aboriginality would be free of problems or controversy. One can imagine, for example, a situation wherein reasonable people may disagree about the specific rights that would be required in order to protect a nation-to-nation version of the collective identity. In other words, agreement on which version of aboriginality is to be the object of constitutional protection does not guarantee that there will be no debate about the proper scope of the requisite rights. However, it is my view that such a situation (a single, clear disagreement about the scope of a set of rights) is an improvement over our current predicament (a convoluted disagreement about the proper scope of rights, when the parties also disagree about what, exactly, the rights should protect). A good argument for using the nation-to-nation conception of aboriginality instead of the citizen-state conception is that, if rights are going to create problems for the rights-holder, then it is only proper that the rights-holder should have a significant say in the nature and scope of those rights. As the analysis demonstrates, this is not currently the case for Aboriginal peoples in Canada. For those reasons, I put forward that employing a nation-to-nation conception is the best we can do if we continue to follow the court's lead and maintain the link between aboriginality and section 35.

This qualification about the link between aboriginality and section 35 is important, because basing section 35 on a nation-to-nation conception of aboriginality does not necessarily lead to Aboriginal peoples being treated fairly. In particular, rights that protect Aboriginal self-definition and self-government could, in principle, still allow for the continued existence of the mechanisms of Aboriginal subordination in Canada outlined above (i.e., the Crown's sovereignty, title, and the like). I do not argue that the mechanisms would not be altered by such a change – indeed, they may be altered in significant ways. What I argue is that there is no guarantee that they would change to such a degree that they would no longer be a problem (either in theory or in practice) for Aboriginal peoples. A better course – if the goal is to create rights that are capable of addressing the unfair treatment of Aboriginal peoples – is to focus on the mechanisms of subordination when constructing rights, thus shifting the concern from identity to things such as the Crown's sovereignty and title. The result would be an uncoupling of Aboriginal rights from aboriginality.

There is some good, scholarly work that supports this proposition. For example, Caroline Dick (2006) goes a long way to illustrating how the link between aboriginality and rights can facilitate intra-group oppression and domination. She calls on us to separate Aboriginal rights from aboriginality. Moreover, the case against the connection of Aboriginal rights and aboriginality may be generalizable – that is, it may simply be unwise to link group rights to identity. While I do not present the case for this argument in this book, I am of the view that the analysis presented herein could certainly be of use for scholars and political practitioners interested in advancing such an argument.

In terms of a way forward – that is, the question of what to do if Aboriginal rights were decoupled from aboriginality – we could look back to the 1980s, to the constitutionally mandated meetings on section 35. While the meetings ended with no agreement, perhaps it is time to reconsider the position advanced by the Aboriginal participants (i.e., that the principle of self-determination ought to anchor section 35). The resulting conversation would be characterized by questions such as: What types of rights would come out of a constitutional provision premised on the principle of Aboriginal self-determination? How would such an alteration to section 35 change the relationship between the Crown and Aboriginal nations? Would these changes ameliorate the daily lived experiences of Aboriginal peoples? I do not have any concrete answers to these questions, but I think it would be worthwhile to have this conversation. My suspicion is that as long as section 35 remains firmly anchored to aboriginality, this conversation remains purely academic; and, unfortunately, so does the just treatment of Aboriginal peoples living in Canada.

Litigation, Political Negotiations, and Reconciliation

One may wonder (quite understandably) whether overreliance on litigation contributed to the problems plaguing section 35 rights. Perhaps political negotiations would have been a better way for Aboriginal peoples and the state to develop rights that are capable of protecting the important interests held by Aboriginal peoples. In fact, there is a strong consensus in many sectors that political negotiations are the best way for Aboriginal and non-Aboriginal communities to work out most, if not all, of their outstanding conflicts.

For their part, the courts also promote this proposition. In a number of judgments pertaining to Aboriginal rights, the SCC has clearly stated a preference for political negotiations. Legal scholar John J. Borrows's (2003, 244–45) thorough examination of the impact of section 35 surveys numerous examples of SCC justices urging the Aboriginal participants and the Crown to engage in political negotiations instead of resorting to litigation.[3] According to Borrows (2003, 244), the SCC's position results from "the Court's disquiet with having to resolve complex legal issues when the parties have done so little to provide concrete and specific statutory or contractual terms for the Court to interpret." This leads him to observe that "it is plain that the Court would prefer not to deal with these issues as the first line of authority on Aboriginal Rights. The Court would rather perform a subsidiary role in reinforcing the independent political actions of the parties" (Borrows 2003, 244). The problem, he argues, is that political authorities have performed poorly in their efforts to pursue political settlements with Aboriginal peoples and to promote the societal change necessary to facilitate the political solutions that would be acceptable to both Aboriginal and non-Aboriginal Canadians (Borrows 2003, 246, 249).[4] As a consequence, Borrows advises those of us who are interested in achieving inter-societal reconciliation to shift our attention and efforts away from section 35 specifically and constitutional change generally, and instead to focus on societal change and political negotiations. He cautions that "Section 35 can blind us to what needs to be accomplished, even as we think it is opening up a whole new world" (Borrows 2003, 248). He sums up his argument by stating that "to think that s.35 will shoulder the burden of reconciling Aboriginal Peoples with the Crown is to think that our *Constitution* does more than it does" (Borrows 2003, 248).[5]

Borrows builds a convincing case that significant work is required by government and other societal actors if the reconciliation of Aboriginal and non-Aboriginal communities is to become a reality in Canada. Upon first glance, his case seems to coincide with the argument outlined in this book – namely, that the courts have done an inadequate job of working out the meaning of Aboriginal rights. However, even though there may be some overlap that results from the shared belief that political settlements are preferable to litigation, I do not share Borrows's contention that too much attention is focused on the courts and the Constitution. In fact, I take the position that scholars who are interested in inter-societal recon-ciliation and political negotiations ought to keep the SCC and section 35 squarely in their line of sight. This is because, even though the SCC has expressed its preference for negotiated settlement, it has also expressed the opinion that it has a role to play in both inter-societal reconciliation and political negotiations. This role is best characterized as that of facilitator. While Borrows makes a significant effort to highlight the need for political negotiations and societal change (a need that is not disputed here), he seems to ignore the possible negative impact of the SCC on both.

The SCC has encouraged the parties in section 35 cases to engage in political negotiation, while simultaneously promoting the idea that it has a role to play in these negotiations. For example, in *Sparrow*, the SCC concluded that section 35 "provides a solid constitutional base upon which subsequent negotiations can take place."[6] Right from the initial forays into section 35 interpretation, then, the SCC presented the idea that its judgments regarding Aboriginal rights would have a significant role in future negotiations between Aboriginal peoples and the state. To use the SCC's words, these judgments form a constitutional base for future negotiations.

The SCC's decision in the *Delgamuukw* case provides further support for this position. The majority's decision stated:

> the Crown is under a moral, if not legal, duty to enter into and conduct
> those negotiations in good faith. Ultimately, it is through negotiated
> settlements, with good faith and give and take on all sides, reinforced by
> the judgments of this Court, that we will achieve what I state in Van der
> Peet ... to be the basic purpose of s.35(1) – "the reconciliation of the

pre-existence of aboriginal societies with the sovereignty of the Crown." Let us face it, we are all here to stay.[7]

The court put forward that reconciliation through negotiated settlement would be "reinforced by the judgments of this Court." Again, the notion that the SCC can and does facilitate political settlements comes to the fore.

Of course, Borrows is not oblivious to this point. Indeed, he acknowledges that the SCC's approach to section 35 includes the idea that the SCC plays a facilitator role. He states that

> the Court's ability to untangle threats to the country's political stability and civic peace is tempered by their recognition that they are not the best party to ultimately work out the details of the necessary arrangements. Thus, they have approached the issue of social cohesion in questions of Aboriginal citizenship by devising procedures and broad principles to direct the parties in better performing their duties in this regard." (Borrows 2003, 249)

According to Borrows, the SCC has indicated that it has a role to play in negotiations between Aboriginal peoples and the state because it provides structural support for the negotiations in the form of procedures and broad principles that guide the parties.

The notion that the SCC and section 35 jurisprudence impact either political negotiations or inter-societal reconciliation should be of concern to all Canadians given the analysis presented in this book.[8] What kind of political negotiations or inter-societal reconciliation could be supported by the SCC and its jurisprudence on Aboriginal rights? Given that the SCC employs a citizen-state conception of aboriginality in its characterization of Aboriginal rights, it is likely that the body of existing jurisprudence on Aboriginal rights would only be capable of supporting political settlements and societal change that advanced a citizen-state conception of aboriginality. One of the main goals of this book is to demonstrate that rights based on the citizen-state conception are unable to protect the nation-to-nation conception of aboriginality. And in my view, negotiations and societal change that produced the same result (i.e., that do not result in the protection of Aboriginal peoples' collective identities as they understand them) would probably frustrate, if not render impossible, the achievement of inter-societal reconciliation. Along the same lines, this book highlights the serious problems that result from the fact that section 35 rights protect the citizen-state conception of aboriginality. Negotiations and societal change that are premised on a citizen-state conception may result in similar harms, inducing Aboriginal peoples to reject inter-societal reconciliation, just as some have rejected section 35 rights (Alfred 2005, 24).

It does not make any sense, then, to shift our attention away from this constitutional provision, as Borrows suggests – the stakes are far too high. The better course of action would be to continue to scrutinize and critically assess section 35 jurisprudence and the impact of the SCC on efforts to reach political settlements and achieve inter-societal reconciliation. Failing to do so may eliminate the benefits of any future political settlements and, in the process, place inter-societal reconciliation even further out of our reach.

Conclusion

I began this book by analyzing the link often drawn between rights and justice in the academic literature. It is my hope that nothing in this book would lead one to reject the claim that respecting people's rights is part of what it means to treat them justly. I wholeheartedly agree with this claim. My aim in writing this book is to illustrate just how difficult it can be to put this seemingly simple claim about rights and justice into practice.

The case of Aboriginal peoples living in Canada is an interesting and informative one. Before Aboriginal rights were recognized in the *Constitution Act, 1982*, many non-Aboriginal Canadians rejected the idea that Aboriginal peoples had group-specific rights. For a variety of reasons, many non-Aboriginal Canadians believed that treating Aboriginal Canadians justly was compatible with denying the existence of Aboriginal rights (Turner 2006, 34–35). In 1982, after a long and hard-fought campaign by Aboriginal peoples, their organizations, and their non-Aboriginal allies, Aboriginal rights finally received constitutional recognition in section 35. This development was certainly worthy of celebration.

And yet, the recognition of Aboriginal rights in Canada has yet to bring about the just treatment of Aboriginal peoples. The lead-up to the inclusion of Aboriginal rights in the Constitution and the events that took place after the *Constitution Act, 1982*, received royal assent contributed to this disappointing outcome. Due to the politics of the day, it was decided in 1982 that the question of the precise nature of Aboriginal rights would be settled after the new constitution became the law of the land, at a series of high-level conferences that took place between 1983 and 1987. During the conferences, the federal, provincial, and Aboriginal participants failed to reach an agreement on the matter. As is so often the case when political processes break down and conflicts are left unresolved, the concerned parties turned to the courts. Thus, by the end of the 1980s, it became clear to most parties that the courts would be called upon to determine the meaning of Aboriginal rights in Canada. Since its first section 35 decision in 1990, the Supreme Court of Canada has come under intense scrutiny regarding its Aboriginal rights jurisprudence, and it has been the subject of significant criticism from multiple quarters.

This book adds to the mounting criticism. Its critical case, however, is distinctive. The analysis in this book brings together scholarship on Aboriginal politics, the law, and philosophy in order to illustrate how the court's decision to connect Aboriginal rights to aboriginality is problematic. Specifically, the analysis demonstrates that Aboriginal rights are constructed to protect the citizen-state version of aboriginality – the understanding of aboriginality held by the justices of the Supreme Court of Canada. This conception of the collective identity is quite different from the nation-to-nation conception consistently put forward by the Aboriginal participants involved in section 35 litigation. This result is far from ideal for Aboriginal peoples and leads to a number of serious consequences.

First, rights constructed to protect the citizen-state conception are poor instruments for protecting the nation-to-nation conception of aboriginality. And as the analysis reveals, when protection of Aboriginal peoples' identity-based interests does occur, it occurs only indirectly. It occurs because a specific identity-based interest of a particular Aboriginal group happens to be compatible with the citizen-state conception of the collective identity. Demanding this type of compatibility as a condition of accommodation is unfair.

Second, the court fails to provide reasons for its decision to protect the citizen-state conception of aboriginality. This creates a jurisprudential justification gap that undermines the legitimacy of the court's section 35 jurisprudence and fails to treat Aboriginal peoples with the requisite degree of respect. Aside from this serious shortcoming, the analysis illustrates that section 35 as it is currently constructed harms Aboriginal peoples in two basic ways. It misrecognizes them by basing Aboriginal rights on a conception of aboriginality that they do not advance (i.e., the citizen-state conception). It also treats Aboriginal peoples unfairly by demanding that they accept as legitimate the Crown's sovereignty and title, two primary causes of Aboriginal subordination in Canada.

The analysis in this book advances that, if the court continues to insist that section 35 should be connected to aboriginality, Aboriginal rights should be reconstructed to protect the nation-to-nation conception. While I believe this would be an improvement over the current state of affairs because the harm of misrecognition and the jurisprudential justification gap would disappear, I argue that protecting the nation-to-nation conception would not necessarily guarantee that Aboriginal people would be treated fairly. Challenges revolving around the nature and scope of the Crown's sovereignty and title would still remain.

In their work on Aboriginal rights and political theory, Duncan Ivison, Paul Patton, and Will Sanders (2000, 3) advance that rights are best understood as instruments whose raison d'être is the protection of fundamental human interests. From their view, rights "appeal to conceptions of what counts as a fundamental interest and are shaped by the particular contexts and challenges faced in securing or promoting those interests" (Ivison, Patton, and Sanders 2000, 3). In this book, we see how the misidentification of these interests (which is reflected in the court's decision to link section 35 rights to identity) results in a set of rights that not only accomplishes less than Aboriginal peoples need or deserve but that also threatens the very interests that Aboriginal peoples consider fundamental. If the goal is to create a just future, the role that such a set of rights would play is certainly in doubt. Assuming that we do not want to abandon this goal and that we still maintain a belief in the link between justice and rights, then we need to rethink Aboriginal rights in Canada and the interests they are meant to protect.

Notes

Introduction

1 Rainbolt (1993, 98) makes the point thus: "If P1 has a claim wrt P2, then P2 has a duty wrt P1 and so P2 has a normative constraint wrt her actions," where "P" stands for "person" and "wrt" means "with respect to."

2 The distinction I draw between sufficient and conclusive reasons is commonly employed by political philosophers (Gilbert 2006, 31). When we say that one has a sufficient reason to do something, what we are saying is that one does not require any additional reasons for doing that thing. This does not mean, however, that it is impossible to come up with a reason that may lead one not to do the thing in question. By contrast, when we say that one has a conclusive reason for doing something, what we are saying is that one does not require any additional reasons, and no reason could be offered for not doing the thing in question.

3 According to Kymlicka (1995, 76), a societal culture provides people with "meaningful ways of life across the full range of human activities, including social, educational, religious, recreational, and economic life, encompassing both public and private spheres."

4 Kymlicka (1995) argues that, in general, polyethnic groups and subnational minority groups are entitled to group-differentiated rights; however, the exact bundle of rights each group can legitimately claim is context specific and variable. Broadly speaking, polyethnic groups are entitled to polyethnic rights such as policies and programs that aim to eliminate discrimination, state funding for minority cultural practices, and group-specific exemptions from certain laws and policies (ibid., 30–31). Subnational minority groups are entitled to self-government rights, which are generally meant to entail some jurisdictional

authority over members of subnational minority groups and their claimed homelands (ibid., 27). And both polyethnic and subnational minority groups are entitled to special representation rights that aim to increase the participation of members of the nonmajority group in society's important political institutions such as legislatures and courts (ibid., 31–33).

5 *R. v. Sparrow*, [1990] 1 S.C.R. 1075 [*Sparrow*].

Chapter 1: The Historical and Legal Framework for Section 35

1 *St. Catherine's Lumber & Milling Co. v. The Queen*, [1888], 14 App. Cas. 46 (J.C.P.C.).

2 *Calder et al. v. Attorney-General of British Columbia* [1973], S.C.R. 313 [*Calder*].

3 Some argue that characterizing the *Calder* case as a loss for Aboriginal peoples is not accurate. Indeed, when the SCC handed down its decision, Aboriginal activist and intellectual George Manuel (quoted in Manuel and Posluns 1974, 223) argued that the *Calder* case represented an Aboriginal "win" since half of the judges who mentioned Aboriginal rights/native title "favoured recognition and found that there was a sound basis in the law of Canada and Britain for recognition."

4 *Constitution Act, 1982*, being Schedule B to the *Canada Act 1982* (UK), 1982, c. 11, s. 35, (1)–(4).

5 The British Parliament passed the *Constitution Act, 1940*, so that the Canadian government could act on unemployment insurance, and the *British North America Act, 1951* so that it could act on pensions.

6 According to Russell (2004, 4), by the early part of the twentieth century, the British were already signalling their willingness to eliminate their role in Canadian constitutional affairs. He argues that Great Britain made this clear by declaring Canada (as well as four other commonwealth states) an "autonomous community" during the imperial conference of 1926.

7 For an informative and extensive empirical study of these constitutionally mandated meetings, see David Hawkes' *Aboriginal Peoples and Constitutional Reform: What Have We Learned?* (1989).

8 *R. v. Badger*, [1996] 1 S.C.R. 771 at para. 76.

9 *Sparrow* at 11.

10 Ibid. at 32.

11 Ibid. at 37–38.

12 Ibid. For a comprehensive list of the factors offered by the court, consult *Sparrow* at 37–38; and *R. v. Gladstone*, [1996] 2 S.C.R. 723 [*Gladstone*] at para. 75.

13 *R. v. Van der Peet*, [1996] 2 S.C.R. 507 [*Van der Peet*].

14 Ibid. at para. 19.

15 Ibid. at para. 20.

16 Ibid.

17 Ibid. at para. 30.

18 Ibid. at para. 27.

19 Ibid. at para. 45.

20 *R. v. Sappier; R. v. Gray*, [2006] 2 S.C.R. 686, 2006 SCC 54 [*Sappier; Gray*] at para. 22.

21 *Van der Peet* at para. 46.

22 Ibid. at para. 71.

23 Ibid. at paras. 55-56.

24 Ibid. at para. 56.

25 *Van der Peet* at para. 60; *R. v. Powley*, [2003] 2 S.C.R. 207, 2003 SCC 43 [*Powley*] at paras. 16-18, 36-40. For academic commentary on the different temporal requirements for a successful Aboriginal rights claim, see the works of Stevenson (2003), Wilkins (2004, 309), and Bell (2003).

26 *Van der Peet* at para. 73.

27 *Delgamuukw v. British Columbia*, [1997] 3 S.C.R. 1010 [*Delgamuukw*] at paras. 172-83.

28 *Sappier; Gray* at para. 57.

29 *Sparrow* at 39. Legal scholar Douglas Lambert (2009, 40) explains the court's interest in these matters thus: "Those tests are designed to ask whether the interference with the right is so minor as to be unworthy of the law's attention. If it makes no difference to the exercise of the right it probably will not be an infringement." From Lambert's view, consideration of these factors is a way to differentiate between action that constitutes an infringement that we should be concerned about and action that does not constitute an infringement or that does constitute an infringement but that is not worthy of our concern.

30 *Sparrow* at 40.

31 *Delgamuukw*, held: 1021-22.

32 Some scholars question the logical coherence of, on the one hand, the recognition that the Crown is in a fiduciary relationship with Aboriginal peoples and, on the other hand, the Crown's ability to infringe Aboriginal rights. Borrows (2003, 235) writes, "It is somewhat ironic that a doctrine, which has been used to protect Aboriginal Peoples from the arbitrary power of government (the fiduciary obligation), was turned on its head and used as a justification for infringing constitutionally protected Aboriginal Rights." He goes on to explain how the SCC's concern for social cohesion and social peace renders

intelligible (though not justifiable) this contradiction (ibid.). McNeil (2001, 319) offers a similar account for this apparent inconsistency: "How any infringement of Aboriginal rights can accommodate the Crown's fiduciary duty is somewhat of a puzzle, as it seems to violate the basic principle that a fiduciary is bound to act in the best interests of the person(s) to whom the duty is owed. Perhaps the explanation is that the Crown has other obligations (e.g. to the Canadian public generally) that can conflict with the duty owed to Aboriginal people so the duty has to be tempered for that reason. This is achieved in part by describing the Crown/Aboriginal relationship as sui generis ... permitting the courts to apply fiduciary principles with flexibility."

33 *Sparrow* at 1108.
34 For example, *St. Ann's Island Hunting And Fishing Club Ltd. v. R.*, [1950] S.C.R. 211; *Guerin v. R*, [1984], 2 S.C.R. 335.
35 *Haida Nation v. British Columbia (Minister of Forests)*, [2004] 3 S.C.R. 511, 2004 SCC 73 [*Haida Nation*]; *Mikisew Cree First Nation v. Canada (Minister of Heritage)*, [2005] 3 S.C.R. 388, 2005 SCC 69 [*Mikisew Cree*]; *Rio Tinto Alcan Inc. v. Carrier Sekani Tribal Council*, 2010 SCC 43, [2010] 2. S.C.R. 650 [*Rio Tinto*]; *Taku River Tlingit First Nation v. British Columbia (Project Assessment Director)*, [2004] 3 S.C.R. 550, 2004 SCC 74 [*Taku River*]; *Tsilhqot'in Nation v. British Columbia*, [2014] SCC 44 [*Tsilhqot'in*].
36 *Taku River* at paras. 43–44.
37 *Tsilhqot'in* at para. 79.
38 *Tsilhqot'in* clarified a number of important issues related to Aboriginal title. For example, it settled the debate about whether nomadic and semi-nomadic peoples could claim this title; it specified what "occupancy" means in more detail, as well as the type of evidence that can be used to prove occupancy; and it rejected the argument that the boundaries of Aboriginal title are limited to settled or semi-settled land (i.e., the "postage stamp" view) (Luk 2014).
39 *Delgamuukw* at para. 1.
40 Ibid. at para. 117.
41 *Tsilhqot'in* at para. 67.
42 Ibid. at para. 25.
43 Ibid.
44 Ibid. at para. 50.
45 Ibid. at para. 46.
46 Ibid. at para. 48.
47 Ibid.
48 Ibid. at para. 50.

49 Ibid.

50 *Delgamuukw* at para. 117.

51 The tests for demonstrating prima facie infringement were outlined in cases involving activity-based rights – *Sparrow* and *Van der Peet* – as opposed to Aboriginal title. Lambert (2009) argues that, in Aboriginal title cases, these tests must be (and have been) modified.

52 *Delgamuukw* at para. 168.

53 Ibid. at para. 169.

54 Ibid. at para. 115.

55 Ibid. at para. 114.

56 Ibid. at para. 113.

57 Ibid. at para. 111.

58 For an earlier, though more narrow, version of this argument, see my 2007 article, "The Plurality of Meanings Shouldered by the Term 'Aboriginality': An Analysis of the Delgamuukw Case" (Panagos 2007).

Chapter 2: Competing Approaches and Conceptualizations of Aboriginality

1 Indeed, I do not include (or spend a great deal of time on) a number of perspectives on aboriginality that are quite important in the scholarly literature – the most significant of the overlooked perspectives being what critical theorists (e.g., Lange 1998) and postcolonialists (e.g., Alfred 1999) have to say about the Aboriginal collective identity. I leave out these traditions only because they are not present in the court material (i.e., no participant in the section 35 cases I examine advanced a conception of aboriginality that mirrors the ones generally advanced in these traditions).

2 Flanagan (2000, 34) is careful to point out that he does not employ the term "civilized" in a normatively critical sense. He explains that "the use of the term [civilization] here is a factual, not a normative concept. It describes a certain type of social organization that has gradually emerged and spread around the entire world. It is not that savagery is bad and civilization is good; both are stages of social development that have arisen sequentially in the historical process." I include this qualification here even though I do not accept Flanagan's argument regarding the neutrality of the term.

Chapter 3: The Case for a Relational Approach

1 Additional critiques of contractarianism include work by Charles Mills (1997), on contracts and racism, and by Robert Nichols (2013), on contracts and settler state colonialism.

2 For a compelling defence of epistemic privilege, see Satya P. Mohanty's (2000) "The Epistemic Status of Cultural Identity: On *Beloved* and the Postcolonial Condition."

3 What Dick (2011) refers to as the Sawridge dispute includes a number of cases that made their way through the courts beginning in the 1990s and ending in 2009: *Sawridge Band v. Canada*, [1996] 1 F.C. 3 (F.C.T.D.); *Sawridge Band v. Canada*, [1997] 3 F.C. 580 (F.C.A.); *Sawridge Band v. Canada*, (1999) 164 F.T.R. 95 (F.C.T.D.); *Sawridge Band v. Canada*, [2003] 3 C.N.L.R. 344 (F.C.T.D.); *Sawridge Band v. Canada*, [2003] F.C. 1083 (F.C.T.D.); *Sawridge First Nation v. Canada*, 2009 FCA 123 (F.C.A.).

4 *An Act to Amend the Indian Act*, R.S.C., 1985 (1st Supp.), c.32.

Chapter 4: The Nation-to-Nation, Colonial, and Citizen-State Approaches

1 Europeans and Aboriginal peoples may have interacted in a noncoercive fashion for other reasons. For example, some argue that Aboriginal beliefs (specifically those concerning sharing and care) underpinned these cooperative interactions (Tully 2008, 244–45). For our purposes, the motivation for the cooperative interactions is less important than the nature of the interactions themselves.

2 By work, I mean state projects such as the provision of welfare or mobilization in times of crisis or war. Scholars such as Barry (2001) argue that ethnocultural diversity can diminish citizens' feelings of solidarity, which erodes support for the welfare state and policies of redistribution.

3 For an explicit statement concerning Cairns's rejection of treaty federalism, see "The Aboriginal Peoples' Movement and Its Critics" by Larry N. Chartrand (2003, 465–66). For a comprehensive and compelling presentation of the meaning, historical and conceptual origins, and implications of treaty federalism, see "Empowering Treaty Federalism" by James Youngblood Henderson (1994). For an analysis of treaty federalism in practice in Canada, see "Treaty Federalism in Northern Canada: Aboriginal-Government Land Claims Boards" by Graham White (2002).

Chapter 5: Submissions to the Court

1 The most important cases include, but are not limited to, *Sparrow*; *Van der Peet*; *Gladstone*; *R. v. Adams*, [1996] 3 S.C.R. 101; *R. v. Marshall, R. v. Bernard*, [2005] 2 S.C.R. 220, 2005 SCC 43 [*Marshall; Bernard*]; and *Haida Nation*.

2 *Sparrow* (Factum of the Appellant, Ronald Edward Sparrow, at para. 2).

3 *Sparrow* (Factum of the Intervener, National Indian Brotherhood / Assembly of First Nations, at para. 1).

4 *Van der Peet* (Factum of the Appellant, Dorothy Marie Van der Peet, at para. 107).

5 Ibid.

6 *Delgamuukw* (Factum of the Appellant, Wet'suwet'en Hereditary Chiefs, at para. 139).

7 Ibid. at para. 156.

8 Ibid. at para. 137.

9 *Delgamuukw* (Factum of the Appellant, Gitksan Hereditary Chiefs, at para. 39).

10 Ibid. at para. 108.

11 *Van der Peet* (Factum of the Appellant, Dorothy Marie Van der Peet, at para. 8).

12 Ibid. at para. 10.

13 Ibid. at para. 105.

14 *Sparrow* (Factum of the Intervener, National Indian Brotherhood/Assembly of First Nations, at para. 17).

15 *Delgamuukw* (Factum of the Appellant, Gitksan Hereditary Chiefs, at para. 78).

16 *Delgamuukw* (Factum of the Appellant, Wet'suwet'en Hereditary Chiefs, at para. 56).

17 *R. v. Pamajewon*, [1996] 2 S.C.R. 821 [*Pamajewon*].

18 *Pamajewon* (Factum of the Intervener, Federation of Saskatchewan Indians and White Bear First Nations, at para. 13).

19 Ibid. See also *Delgamuukw* (Factum of the Appellant, Gitksan Hereditary Chiefs, at 58-59, para. 223).

20 *Delgamuukw* (Factum of the Intervener, Westbank First Nation, at para. 42).

21 *Pamajewon* (Factum of the Appellants, Pamajewon and Jones, at para. 23).

22 *Pamajewon* (Factum of the Intervener, Federation of Saskatchewan Indians and White Bear First Nations, at para. 16). See also *Delgamuukw* (Factum of the Appellant, Wet'suwet'en Hereditary Chiefs, at 54, para. 160).

23 *Delgamuukw* (Factum of the Appellant, Gitksan Hereditary Chiefs, at para. 208).

24 *Pamajewon* (Factum of the Appellants, Pamajewon and Jones, at para. 64).

25 Ibid. at para. 65.

26 *Sparrow* (Factum of the Intervener, National Indian Brotherhood/Assembly of First Nations, at para. 20).

27 Ibid.

28 *Sparrow* (Factum of the Respondent, HMQ, Attorney General of Canada at para. 89).

29 Ibid.

30 *Sparrow* (Factum of the Attorney General of British Columbia, at para. 34).

31 *Van der Peet* (Factum of the Respondent, HMQ, at para. 14).

32 Ibid. at para. 15.

33 *Gladstone* (Factum of the Respondent, HMQ, at para. 77).

34 Ibid. at para. 112. For a similar view on the noncommercial aspect of harvesting rights, see *Sappier; Gray* at para. 25.

35 *Pamajewon* (Factum of the Respondent, the Attorney General of Ontario, at para. 11).

36 *Delgamuukw* (Factum of the Appellant, Wet'suwet'en Hereditary Chiefs, at para. 137); *Delgamuukw* (Factum of the Appellant, Gitksan Hereditary Chiefs, at paras. 14–15, 36–37).

37 *Delgammukw* (Factum of the Attorney General of Canada at para. 136).

38 Ibid. at para. 131.

39 *Delgammukw* (Factum of the Attorney General of British Columbia at para. 299).

40 Ibid. at para. 294.

41 *Delgamuukw* (Factum of the Appellant, Wet'suwet'en Hereditary Chiefs, at para. 56).

42 *Gladstone* (Factum of the Attorney General of Alberta at para. 13).

43 *Delgamuukw* (Factum of the Attorney General of British Columbia at para. 140).

44 *Pamajewon* (Factum of the Respondent, the Attorney General of Ontario, at para. 14).

45 *Sparrow* (Factum of the Attorney General of Alberta at para. 6).

46 *Mitchell v. M.N.R.*, [2001] 1 S.C.R. 911, 2001 SCC 33 [*Mitchell*].

47 *Mitchell* (Factum of the Appellant, the Minister of National Revenue, at para. 1).

48 *Pamajewon* (Factum of the Intervener, the Attorney General of Canada, at para. 2).

49 Ibid. at para. 7.

Chapter 6: What the Justices Said

1 *Van der Peet* at para. 19.

2 Ibid.

3 Ibid. at para. 30.

4 Ibid. at para. 44.

5 Ibid. at para. 45.

6 *Mitchell* at para. 12.

7 Ibid.

8 *Powley* at para. 13.

9 *Sparrow* at 30.

10 *Van der Peet* at para. 31.

11 *Delgamuukw* at para. 128.

12 Ibid.

13 Ibid. at para. 125.

14 Ibid at para. 127.

15 *Mitchell* at para. 132.

16 Ibid. at para. 133.

17 *Gladstone* at para. 73.

18 *Sparrow* at 37–38; *Gladstone* at para. 75.

19 For a list of these objectives, consult the following cases: *Sparrow* at 37–38 and *Gladstone* at para. 75. For academic commentary on these objectives and their impact on section 35 rights, see "Defining Aboriginal Title in the 90's: Has the Supreme Court Finally Got It Right?" by Kent McNeil (1998), and "Domesticating Doctrines: Aboriginal Peoples after the Royal Commission" by John J. Borrows (2001, 647–49).

20 The entire citation reads: "It could be said that Aboriginal Peoples were claiming that social cohesion and civil peace under s.35(1) would best be served through a recognition of their ability to exercise regulatory authority in Canada in a manner similar, though with obvious differences, to that shared by the Dominion and provincial governments" (Borrows 2003, 233).

21 After all, any kind of change in the proprietary power and legislative authority of the Crown that went above and beyond "a marginal shift" would surely have political implications for the broader pan-Canadian community. Along the same lines, altering the Crown's current role in authorizing and regulating third-party use of Crown land (which includes Aboriginal peoples' traditional territories) would have a substantial economic impact in various parts of the country. For some interesting analysis of the relationship between the Crown's interest in maintaining the current political and economic status quo and the subsequent limits on Aboriginal title and Aboriginal self-government, see the works of Rynard (2001), Niezen (2003a, 8–9, 22–25), and Stevenson (1998, 42, 46).

Chapter 7: Aboriginal Rights Jurisprudence and Identity Contestation

1 *Sparrow* at 30.

2 According to legal scholar Jennifer E. Dalton (2006, 17), the court has made similar statements about the importance of the sovereignty of the Crown in other important cases, including *Van der Peet* and *Gladstone*.

3 For example, in the *Charter of the United Nations*, Article 1, para. 2 and Article 55.

4 The point here is not that these activities should be permitted. The point is that they are not allowed, even if the Aboriginal group wanted to pursue such a type of land use.

5. For additional critique of a practice- or culture-based approach to section 35 rights, see works by Gordon Christie (2003, 484), Caroline Dick (2009), and Michael Murphy (2001b).

Chapter 8: A Problematic Conception of Rights

1 *R. v. Sheppard*, [2002] 1 S.C.R. 869, 2002 SCC 26.

2 Carens (2003) is referring specifically to requiring members of a minority group to conform to a majority group's culture and society. However, the point is equally valid in this instance (that is, requiring them to conform to a version of their culture and identity that they do not hold). This equivalency can be drawn because, in both cases, the culture and identity are alien to the group in question.

3 Borrows (2003) cites the following cases as evidence of the SCC's encouragement of negotiations: *Delgamuukw*; *Sparrow*; *R. v. Sioui*, [1990] 1 S.C.R. 1025; *R. v. Horseman*, (1990), 1 S.C.R. 901 (S.C.C.) [*Horseman*]; *Lovelace v. Ontario*, [2000] 1 S.C.R. 950 [*Lovelace*]; and *C.P. v. Matsqui Indian Band*, [1995] 1 S.C.R. 3 [*Matsqui Indian Band*]. See also *Haida Nation*, paras. 14, 38; *R. v. Marshall*, [1993] 3 S.C.R. 533, para. 22. For an analysis of the SCC's support for political negotiations, see "The Sparrow Doctrine: Beginning of the End or End of the Beginning?" (Binnie 1990, 221, 242). For an analysis of Aboriginal title and the SCC's call for negotiations, see "Domesticating Doctrines: Aboriginal Peoples after the Royal Commission" (Borrows 2001, 644).

4 For example, Borrows (2003, 246) argues that "it is time those in the political arena heeded this message, and bring greater peace and stability to Canada by negotiating for the resolution of those issues that treat at our common humanity. While there have been some efforts and successes in this regard, the unconscionably slow pace at which this is occurring illustrates that there needs to be a broader based concern with concepts of citizenship attentive to our long term interdependencies." He goes on to explain that "Section 35 is a lever, a tool – a platform for further extending the development of a political culture that is supportive of Aboriginal Rights. But the most important work lies beyond this horizon. In the media, classrooms, kitchens, committee rooms, party strategy rooms, union halls, churches, corporate board rooms, cabinet and legislatures of this, and other countries" (ibid., 249).

5 Borrows (2003, 247) reinforces this point by arguing that "we do ourselves a great disservice if all our efforts for reform are channeled through the language and categories of *Constitution* or discussions about Canadian citizenship. The Constitution, by and large, does not cut across the grain of society, but runs with it."

6 *Sparrow* at 1105.

7 *Delgamuukw* at para. 186.

8 Leonard I. Rotman advances that section 35 jurisprudence does in fact impact political negotiations. He argues that "Aboriginal and treaty rights litigation begets negotiation and that negotiations becomes meaningful and effective only with the continued presence, or threat, of litigation" (Rotman 2004, 227).

References

Abele, Frances. 2005. "Belonging in the New World: Imperialism, Property and Citizenship." In *Insiders and Outsiders: Alan Cairns and the Reshaping of Canadian Citizenship*, ed. Gerald Kernerman and Philip Resnick, 213-26. Vancouver: UBC Press.

Alfred, Taiaiake. 1999. *Peace, Power, Righteousness: An Indigenous Manifesto*. Oxford: Oxford University Press.

– 2005. *Wasáse: Indigenous Pathways of Action and Freedom*. Peterborough, ON: Broadview Press.

Alfred, Taiaiake, and Jeff Corntassel. 2005. "Being Indigenous: Resurgences against Contemporary Colonialism." In *Politics of Identity IX*, ed. Richard Bellamy, 597-617. Oxford: Government and Opposition. http://dx.doi.org/10.1111/j.1477-7053.2005.00166.x.

Asch, Michael. 1999. "From Calder to Van der Peet: Aboriginal Rights and Canadian Law, 1973-1996." In *Indigenous Peoples' Rights in Australia, Canada and New Zealand*, ed. Paul Havemann, 428-46. Oxford: Oxford University Press.

Bachvarova, Mira. 2014. "Multicultural Accommodation and the Ideal of Non-Domination." *Critical Review of International Social and Political Philosophy* 17 (6): 652-73.

Barcham, Manuhuia. 2000. "(De)Constructing the Politics of Indigeneity." In *Political Theory and the Rights of Indigenous Peoples*, ed. Duncan Ivison, Paul Patton, and Will Sanders, 137-51. Cambridge: Cambridge University Press.

Barry, Brian. 2001. *Culture and Equality: An Egalitarian Critique of Multiculturalism*. Cambridge: Cambridge University Press.

Barsh, Russel Lawrence, and James Youngblood Henderson. 1997. "The Supreme Court's Van der Peet Trilogy: Naïve Imperialism and Ropes of Sand." *McGill Law Journal/Revue de droit de McGill* 42 (4): 993-1009.

Bell, Catherine. 2003. "Towards an Understanding of Metis Aboriginal Rights: Reflections on the Reasoning in R. v. Powley." In *Aboriginal Rights Litigation*, ed. Joseph Eliot Magnet and Dwight A. Dorey, 387–434. Markham, ON: LexisNexis Canada.

Binnie, W.I.C. 1990. "The Sparrow Doctrine: Beginning of the End or End of the Beginning?" *Queen's Law Journal* 15: 217–53.

Blauner, Robert. 1969. "Internal Colonialism and Ghetto Revolt." *Social Problems* 16 (4): 393–408. http://dx.doi.org/10.2307/799949.

Borrows, John J. 2001. "Domesticating Doctrines: Aboriginal Peoples after the Royal Commission." *McGill Law Journal* 46 (3): 615–61.

– 2002. *Recovering Canada: The Resurgence of Indigenous Law.* Toronto: University of Toronto Press.

– 2003. "Measuring a Work in Progress: Canada, Constitutionalism, Citizenship and Aboriginal Peoples." In *Box of Treasures or Empty Box? Twenty Years of Section 35*, ed. Ardith Walkem and Halie Bruce, 223–62. Penticton, BC: Theytus Books.

– 2010. *Canada's Indigenous Constitution.* Toronto: University of Toronto Press.

Brock, Gillian. 2002. "Are There Any Defensible Indigenous Rights?" *Contemporary Political Theory* 1 (3): 285–305. http://dx.doi.org/10.1057/palgrave.cpt.9300052.

Brubaker, Rogers, and Frederick Cooper. 2000. "Beyond 'Identity.'" *Theory and Society* 29: 1–47.

Bruce, Halie, and Ardith Walkem. 2003. "Bringing Our Living Constitutions Home." In *Box of Treasures or Empty Box? Twenty Years of Section 35*, ed. Ardith Walkem and Halie Bruce, 344–62. Penticton, BC: Theytus Books.

Butler, Judith. 2001. "Doing Justice to Someone: Sex Reassignment and Allegories of Transsexuality." *Journal of Lesbian and Gay Studies* 7 (4): 621–36. http://dx.doi.org/10.1215/10642684-7-4-621.

Cairns, Alan. 2000. *Citizens Plus: Aboriginal Peoples and the Canadian State.* Vancouver: UBC Press.

Canada. 1996. *Report of the Royal Commission on Aboriginal Peoples.* 5 vols. Ottawa: Canada Communication Group Publishing.

Canada, Parliament, Senate. 2007. *Taking Section 35 Seriously: Non-Derogation Clauses Relating to Aboriginal and Treaty Rights.* Standing Committee on Legal and Constitutional Affairs. 2d sess., 39th Parliament. http://www.parl.gc.ca/content/sen/committee/392/lega/rep/rep05dec07-e.pdf.

Cardinal, Harold. 1999. *The Unjust Society.* Vancouver: Douglas and McIntyre.

Carens, Joseph H. 2003. *Culture, Citizenship and Community: A Contextual Exploration of Justice as Evenhandedness.* Oxford Scholarship Online. http://dx.doi.org/10.1093/0198297688.001.0001.

Chambers, Simone. 1998. "Contract Or Conversation: Theoretical Lessons from the Canadian Constitutional Crisis." *Politics and Society* 26 (1): 143–72. http://dx.doi.org/10.1177/0032329298026001006.

Chartrand, Larry N. 2003. "The Aboriginal Peoples' Movement and Its Critics." In *Aboriginal Rights Litigation*, ed. Joseph Eliot Magnet and Dwight A. Dorey, 453–74. Markham, ON: LexisNexis Canada.

Christie, Gordon. 2003. "Aboriginal Citizenship: Sections 35, 25 and 15 of Canada's *Constitution Act, 1982*." *Citizenship Studies* 7 (4): 481–95. http://dx.doi.org/10.1080/1362102032000134994.

– 2004. "Aboriginal Resource Rights after Delgamuukw and Marshall." In *Advancing Aboriginal Claims: Visions/Strategies/Directions*, ed. Kerry Wilkins, 241–70. Saskatoon: Purich Publishing.

– 2007. *Aboriginal Nationhood and the Inherent Right to Self-Government*. National Centre for First Nations Governance (NCFNG). http://fngovernance.org/ncfng_research/gordon_christie.pdf.

Coates, Kenneth, and Dwight Newman. 2014. *The End Is Not Nigh: Reason Over Alarmism in Analysing the Tsilhqot'in Decision*. Ottawa: MacDonald-Laurier Institute.

Coulthard, Glen. 2007. "Subjects of Empire: Indigenous Peoples and the 'Politics of Recognition' in Canada." *Contemporary Political Theory* 6: 437–60. http://dx.doi.org/10.1057/palgrave.cpt.9300307.

Dalton, Jennifer E. 2006. "Aboriginal Self-Determination in Canada: Protections Afforded by the Judiciary and Government." *Canadian Journal of Law and Society* 21 (1): 11–37. http://dx.doi.org/10.1353/jls.2006.0034.

Dhamoon, Rita. 2009. *Identity/Difference Politics: How Difference Is Produced, and Why It Matters*. Vancouver: UBC Press.

Dick, Caroline. 2006. "The Politics of Intragroup Difference: First Nations' Women and the *Sawridge* Dispute." *Canadian Journal of Political Science* 39: 97–116. http://dx.doi.org/10.1017/S0008423906040686.

– 2009. "'Culture and the Courts' Revisited: Group-Rights Scholarship and the Evolution of s.35(1)." *Canadian Journal of Political Science* 42 (4): 957–79.

– 2011. *The Perils of Identity: Group Rights and the Politics of Intragroup Difference*. Vancouver: UBC Press.

Dodson, Michael. 1994. "The End in the Beginning: Re(de)finding Aboriginality." *Australian Aboriginal Studies* 1: 2–13.

Eisenberg, Avigail. 1994. "The Politics of Individual and Group Difference in Canadian Jurisprudence." *Canadian Journal of Political Science* 27: 3–21. http://dx.doi.org/10.1017/S0008423900006193.

Elliott, Mark. 2012. "Has the Common Law Duty to Give Reasons Come of Age Yet?" *University of Cambridge Faculty of Law Research Paper* 7/2012. http://dx.doi.org/10.2139/ssrn.2041362.

Eriksen, Thomas Hylland. 1992. *Us and Them in Modern Societies: Ethnicity and Nationalism in Mauritius, Trinidad and Beyond.* London: Scandinavian University Press.

– 1993. *Ethnicity and Nationalism: Anthropological Perspectives.* London: Pluto Press.

Flanagan, Tom. 2000. *First Nations? Second Thoughts.* Montreal: McGill-Queen's University Press.

Fuss, Diana. 1989. *Essentially Speaking: Feminism, Nature and Difference.* New York: Routledge.

Gilbert, Margaret. 2006. *A Theory of Political Obligation.* Oxford: Oxford University Press.

Goldie, L.F.E. 1985. "Title and Use (and Usufruct): An Ancient Distinction Too Oft Forgot." *American Journal of International Law* 79 (3): 689–714.

Green, Joyce A. 2000. "The Difference Debate: Reducing Rights to Cultural Flavours." *Canadian Journal of Political Science* 33: 133–44. http://dx.doi.org/10.1017/S0008423900000068.

– 2005. "Toward Conceptual Precision: Citizenship and Rights Talk for Aboriginal Canadians." In *Insiders and Outsiders: Alan Cairns and the Reshaping of Canadian Citizenship*, ed. Gerald Kernerman and Philip Resnick, 227–41. Vancouver: UBC Press.

Gutmann, Amy. 1985. "Communitarian Critics of Liberalism." *Philosophy and Public Affairs* 14 (3): 308–22.

– 1994. "Introduction." In *Multiculturalism: Examining the Politics of Recognition*, ed. Amy Gutmann, 3-24. Princeton, NJ: Princeton University Press.

Hamilton, Jonnette Watson. 2014. "Establishing Aboriginal Title: A Return to *Delgamuukw.*" *ABlawg* (blog of the University of Alberta, Faculty of Law), July 2. http://ablawg.ca/2014/07/02/establishing-aboriginal-title-a-return-to-delgamuukw/.

Hanvelt, Marc, and Martin Papillon. 2005. "Parallel Or Embedded? Aboriginal Self-Government and the Changing Nature of Citizenship in Canada." In *Insiders and Outsiders: Alan Cairns and the Reshaping of Canadian Citizenship*, ed. Gerald Kernerman and Philip Resnick, 242–56. Vancouver: UBC Press.

Harris, Douglas. 2009. "A Court Between: Aboriginal and Treaty Rights in the British Columbia Court of Appeal." *BC Studies* 162: 137–64.

Hawkes, David C. 1989. *Aboriginal Peoples and Constitutional Reform: What Have We Learned?* Kingston, ON: Institute of Intergovernmental Relations.

Hayward, Clarissa, and Ron Watson. 2010. "Identity and Political Theory." *Washington University Journal of Law and Policy* 33: 9–41.

Henderson, James Youngblood. 1994. "Empowering Treaty Federalism." *Saskatchewan Law Review* 58 (2): 241–329.

– 1997. "Interpreting Sui Generis Treaties." *Alberta Law Review* 36 (1): 46–96.

Hogg, Peter. 2009. "The Constitutional Basis of Aboriginal Rights." In *Aboriginal Law since Delgamuukw*, ed. Maria Morellato, 3–29. Aurora, ON: Canada Law Group.

Irlbacher-Fox, Stephanie. 2009. *Finding Dahshaa: Self-Government, Social Suffering, and Aboriginal Policy in Canada*. Vancouver: UBC Press.

Ivison, Duncan, Paul Patton, and Will Sanders. 2000. "Introduction." In *Political Theory and the Rights of Indigenous Peoples*, ed. Duncan Ivison, Paul Patton, and Will Sanders, 1–21. Cambridge: Cambridge University Press.

Johnston, Darlene M. 1989. "Native Rights as Collective Rights: A Question of Group Self-Preservation." *Canadian Journal of Law and Jurisprudence* 2 (1): 19–34.

Jung, Courtney. 2003. " 'Indigenous' the New 'Peasant': The Struggle for Political Identity in the Neo-Liberal Age." *Social Research* 70 (2): 1–31.

– 2008. *The Moral Force of Indigenous Politics: Critical Liberalism and the Zapatistas*. New York: Cambridge University Press. http://dx.doi.org/10.1017/CBO9780 511551222.

Kulchyski, Peter. 1994. "Introduction." In *Unjust Relations: Aboriginal Rights in Canadian Courts*, ed. Peter Kulchyski, 1–20. Toronto: Oxford University Press.

Kymlicka, Will. 1995. *Multicultural Citizenship*. Oxford: Oxford University Press.

Ladner, Kiera. 2003. "Rethinking Aboriginal Governance." In *Reinventing Canada*, ed. Janine Brodie and Linda Trimble, 43–60. Toronto: Prentice Hall.

– 2005. "Up the Creek: Fishing for a New Constitutional Order." *Canadian Journal of Political Science* 38 (4): 923–53. http://dx.doi.org/10.1017/S0008423905040539.

Lambert, Douglas. 2009. "Where to from Here: Reconciling Aboriginal Title with Crown Sovereignty." In *Aboriginal Law since Delgamuukw*, ed. Maria Morellato, 31–54. Aurora: Canada Law Book.

Lange, Lynda. 1998. "Burnt Offerings to Rationality: A Feminist Reading of the Construction of Indigenous Peoples in Enrique Dussel's Theory of Modernity." *Hypatia* 13 (3): 132–45. http://dx.doi.org/10.1111/j.1527-2001.1998.tb01374.x.

LaRocque, Emma. 2010. *When the Other Is Me: Native Resistance Discourse, 1850–1990*. Winnipeg: University of Manitoba Press.

Lawrence, Bonita. 2004. *"Real" Indians and Others: Mixed-Blood Urban Native Peoples and Indigenous Nationhood*. Vancouver: UBC Press.

Leclair, Jean. 2006. "Federal Constitutionalism and Aboriginal Difference." *Queen's Law Journal* 31 (2): 521–35.

Levey, Geoffrey Brahm. 1997. "Equality, Autonomy, and Cultural Rights." *Political Theory* 25 (2): 215–48. http://dx.doi.org/10.1177/0090591797025002003.

Levy, Jacob T. 2000. *The Multiculturalism of Fear*. Oxford: Oxford University Press. http://dx.doi.org/10.1093/0198297122.001.0001.

Little Bear, Leroy, Menno Boldt, and J. Anthony Long. 1984. "Indian Government and the Constitution." In *Pathways to Self-Determination: Canadian Indians and the Canadian State*, ed. Leroy Little Bear, Menno Boldt, and J. Anthony Long, 171–80. Toronto: University of Toronto Press.

Luk, Senwung. 2014. "The Law of the Land: New Jurisprudence on Aboriginal Title." *Supreme Court Law Review* 67: 289–317.

Macfarlane, Emmett. 2013. *Governing from the Bench: The Supreme Court of Canada and the Judicial Role*. Vancouver: UBC Press.

Macklem, Patrick. 1997a. "Aboriginal Rights and State Obligations." *Alberta Law Review* 36 (1): 97–116.

– 1997b. "What's Law Got to Do with It? The Protection of Aboriginal Title in Canada." *Osgoode Hall Law Journal* 35: 125–37.

Manuel, Arthur. 2003. "Aboriginal Rights on the Ground: Making Section 35 Meaningful." In *Box of Treasures or Empty Box? Twenty Years of Section 35*, ed Ardith Walkem and Halie Bruce, 316–42. Penticton, BC: Theytus Books.

Manuel, George, and Michael Posluns. 1974. *The Fourth World: An Indian Reality*. New York: Free Press.

Maracle, Lee. 2003. "The Operation Was Successful, but the Patient Died." In *Box of Treasures or Empty Box? Twenty Years of Section 35*, ed. Ardith Walkem and Halie Bruce, 309–15. Penticton, BC: Theytus Books.

McNeil, Kent. 1998. "Defining Aboriginal Title in the 90's: Has the Supreme Court Finally Got It Right?" In *Robarts Lectures*. Toronto: Robarts Centre for Canadian Studies, York University. http://robarts.info.yorku.ca/files/lectures-pdf/rl_mcneil.pdf.

– 2001. *Emerging Justice?: Essays on Indigenous Rights in Canada and Australia*. Saskatoon: Native Law Centre of Canada, University of Saskatchewan.

– 2004a. "Continuity of Aboriginal Rights." In *Advancing Aboriginal Claims: Visions/ Strategies/Directions*, ed. Kerry Wilkins, 127–50. Saskatoon: Purich Publishing.

– 2004b. "The Inherent Right of Self-Government: Emerging Directions for Legal Research." Chilliwack, BC: Centre for First Nations Governance.

Mercredi, Ovide, and Mary Ellen Turpel. 1993. *In the Rapids: Navigating the Future of First Nations*. Toronto: Viking Press.

Miller, Bruce Granville. 2003. *Invisible Indigenes: The Politics of Nonrecognition.* Lincoln, NE: University of Nebraska Press.

Miller, David. 1995. *On Nationality.* Oxford: Clarendon Press.

Miller, J.R. 1989. *Skyscrapers Hide the Heavens: A History of Indian-White Relations in Canada.* Toronto: University of Toronto Press.

–. 2004. *Lethal Legacy: Current Native Controversies in Canada.* Toronto: McClelland and Stewart.

Mills, Charles. 1997. *The Racial Contract.* Ithaca, NY: Cornell University Press.

Mohanty, Satya P. 2000. "The Epistemic Status of Cultural Identity: On *Beloved* and the Postcolonial Condition." In *Reclaiming Identity: Realist Theory and the Predicament of Postmodernism,* ed. Paul M.L. Moya and Michael R. Hames-Garcia, 29–66. Berkeley: University of California Press.

Monture-Angus, Patricia. 1999. *Journeying Forward: Dreaming First Nations' Independence.* Halifax: Fernwood Publishing.

Moore, Margaret. 1997. "On National Self-Determination." *Political Studies* 45 (5): 900–13. http://dx.doi.org/10.1111/1467-9248.00118.

– 2001. *The Ethics of Nationalism.* Oxford: Oxford University Press. http://dx.doi. org/10.1093/0198297467.001.0001.

Morse, Bradford W. 1997. "Permafrost Rights: Aboriginal Self-Government and the Supreme Court in R. v. Pamajewon." *McGill Law Journal/Revue de droit de McGill* 42 (4): 1011–42.

Murphy, Michael. 2001a. "Culture and the Courts: A New Direction in Canadian Jurisprudence on Aboriginal Rights?" *Canadian Journal of Political Science* 34: 109–29.

– 2001b. "The Limits of Culture in the Politics of Self-Determination." *Ethnicities* 1: 367–88. http://dx.doi.org/10.1177/146879680100100305.

– 2006. "Looking Forward Without Looking Back: Jean Chrétien's Legacy for Aboriginal-State Relations." In *The Chrétien Legacy: Politics and Public Policy in Canada,* ed. Lois Harder and Steve Patten, 160–80. Montreal: McGill-Queen's University Press.

Nichols, Robert. 2013. "Indigeneity and the Settler Contract Today." *Philosophy and Social Criticism* 39 (2): 187–208. http://dx.doi.org/10.1177/0191453712470359.

Niezen, Ronald. 2003a. "Culture and the Judiciary: The Meaning of the Culture Concept as a Source of Aboriginal Rights in Canada." *Canadian Journal of Law and Society* 18 (2): 1–26. http://dx.doi.org/10.1017/S0829320100007687.

– 2003b. *The Origins of Indigenism: Human Rights and the Politics of Identity.* Berkeley: University of California Press. http://dx.doi.org/10.1525/california/9780520235540.001.0001.

Nozick, Robert. 1993. *The Nature of Rationality*. Princeton, NJ: Princeton University Press.

Panagos, Dimitrios. 2007. "The Plurality of Meanings Shouldered by the Term 'Aboriginality': An Analysis of the Delgamuukw Case." *Canadian Journal of Political Science* 40 (3): 591–613. http://dx.doi.org/10.1017/S0008423907070710.

Panagos, Dimitrios, and J. Andrew Grant. 2013. "Constitutional Change, Aboriginal Rights, and Mining Policy in Canada." *Commonwealth and Comparative Politics* 51 (4): 405–23. http://dx.doi.org/10.1080/14662043.2013.838373.

Pateman, Carole. 1988. *The Sexual Contract*. Stanford, CA: Stanford University Press.

Perry, Richard J. 1996. *From Time Immemorial: Indigenous Peoples and State Systems*. Austin: University of Texas Press.

Poplar, Mildred C. 2003. "We Were Fighting for Nationhood, Not Section 35." In *Box of Treasures or Empty Box? Twenty Years of Section 35*, ed. Ardith Walkem and Halie Bruce, 23–28. Penticton, BC: Theytus Books.

Rainbolt, George W. 1993. "Rights as Normative Constraints on Others." *Philosophy and Phenomenological Research* 53: 93–111. http://dx.doi.org/10.2307/2108055.

Rawls, John. 1999. *A Theory of Justice*. Rev. ed. Cambridge, MA: Harvard University Press.

Ray, Arthur J. 1996. *I Have Lived Here since the World Began*. Toronto: Lester Publishing.

Razack, Sherene H. 1998. *Looking White People in the Eye: Gender, Race, and Culture in Courtrooms and Classrooms*. Toronto: University of Toronto Press.

– 2004. *Dark Threats and White Knights: The Somalia Affair, Peacekeeping and the New Imperialism*. Toronto: University of Toronto Press.

Rotman, Leonard I. 2004. "Let Us Face It, We Are All Here to Stay: But Do We Negotiate or Litigate?" In *Advancing Aboriginal Claims: Visions/Strategies/Directions*, ed. Kerry Wilkins, 202–40. Saskatoon: Purich Publishing.

Russell, Peter. 2004. *Constitutional Odyssey: Can Canadians Become a Sovereign People?* Toronto: University of Toronto Press.

Rynard, Paul. 2001. "Ally or Colonizer? The Federal State, the Cree Nation and the James Bay Agreement." *Journal of Canadian Studies* 36 (2): 8–48.

Scanlon, T.M. 2002. "Rawls on Justification." In *The Cambridge Companion to Rawls*, ed. Samuel Freeman, 139–67. Cambridge: Cambridge University Press. http://dx.doi.org/10.1017/CCOL0521651670.004.

Scheffler, Samuel. 2001. *Boundaries and Allegiances: Problems of Justice and Responsibility in Liberal Thought*. Oxford: Oxford University Press.

Schouls, Tim. 2003. *Shifting Boundaries: Aboriginal Identity, Pluralist Theory, and the Politics of Self-Government*. Vancouver: UBC Press.

Sealy, L.S. 1962. "Fiduciary Relationships." *Cambridge Law Journal* 20: 69–81. http://dx.doi.org/10.1017/S0008197300086943.

Simmons, A. John. 1999. "Justification and Legitimacy." *Ethics* 109 (4): 739–71. http://dx.doi.org/10.1086/233944.

– 2008. *Political Philosophy*. Oxford: Oxford University Press.

Slattery, Brian. 2005. "Aboriginal Rights and the Honour of the Crown." *Supreme Court Law Review* 29 (2): 433–45.

Stevenson, Mark. 2003. "Section 35 and Metis Aboriginal Rights: Promises Must Be Kept." In *Box of Treasures or Empty Box? Twenty Years of Section 35*, ed. Ardith Walkem and Halie Bruce, 63–102. Princeton, BC: Theytus Books.

Stevenson, Winona. 1998. "'Ethnic' Assimilates 'Inidigenous': A Study in Intellectual Neocolonialism." *Wicazo Sa Review* 31: 33–51.

Taylor, Charles. 1994. "The Politics of Recognition." In *Multiculturalism : Examining the Politics of Recognition*, ed. Amy Gutmann, 25–73. Princeton, NJ: Princeton University Press.

Tully, James. 1995. *Strange Multiplicity: Constitutionalism in an Age of Diversity*. Cambridge: Cambridge University Press. http://dx.doi.org/10.1017/CBO978 1139170888.

– 1999. "Aboriginal Peoples: Negotiating Reconciliation." In *Canadian Politics*, ed. James Bickerton and Alain G. Gagnon, 413–41. Peterborough, ON: Broadview Press.

– 2000a. "The Struggles of Indigenous Peoples for and of Freedom." In *Political Theory and the Rights of Indigenous Peoples*, ed. Duncan Ivision, Paul Patton, and Will Sanders. 36–59. Cambridge: Cambridge University Press.

– 2000b. "Struggles over Recognition and Distribution." *Constellations* 7 (4): 469–82. http://dx.doi.org/10.1111/1467-8675.00203.

– 2008. "The Negotiation of Reconciliation." In *Public Philosophy in a New Key, Volume I: Democracy and Civic Freedom*, ed. James Tully, 223–56. Cambridge: Cambridge University Press.

Turner, Dale. 2006. *This Is Not a Peace Pipe: Towards a Critical Indigenous Philosophy*. Toronto: University of Toronto Press.

Vermette, D'Arcy. 2008. "Colonialism and the Process of Defining Aboriginal Peoples." *Dalhousie Law Journal* 31: 211–46.

– 2011. "Dizzying Dialogue: Canadian Courts and the Continuing Justification of the Dispossession of Aboriginal Peoples." *Windsor Yearbook of Access to Justice* 29: 55–72.

Waddell, Ian. 2003. "Building a Box, Finding Storage Space." In *Box of Treasures or Empty Box? Twenty Years of Section 35*, ed. Ardith Walkem and Halie Bruce, 15–22. Princeton, BC: Theytus Books.

Waldron, Jeremy. 2005. "Nozick and Locke: Filling the Space of Rights." *Social Philosophy and Policy* 22 (1): 81–110. http://dx.doi.org/10.1017/S02650525 0504104X.

Walkem, Ardith. 2003. "Constructing the Constitutional Box: The Supreme Court's Section 35(1) Reasoning." In *Box of Treasures or Empty Box? Twenty Years of Section 35*, ed. Ardith Walkem and Halie Bruce, 196–221. Princeton, BC: Theytus Books.

Walkem, Ardith, and Halie Bruce. 2003. "Introduction." In *Box of Treasures or Empty Box? Twenty Years of Section 35*, ed. Ardith Walkem and Halie Bruce, 9–12. Princeton, BC: Theytus Books.

Watts, Ronald L. 1987. "The American Constitution in Comparative Perspective: A Comparison of Federalism in the United States and Canada." *Journal of American History* 74 (3): 769–92. http://dx.doi.org/10.2307/1902152.

Weinstock, Daniel. 2005. "Beyond Exit Rights: Reframing the Debate." In *Minorities within Minorities: Equality, Rights and Diversity*, ed. Avigail Eisenberg and Jeff Spinner-Halev, 227–47. Cambridge: Cambridge University Press. http://dx.doi. org/10.1017/CBO9780511490224.012.

White, Graham. 2002. "Treaty Federalism in Northern Canada: Aboriginal-Government Land Claims Boards." In *Publius: Journal of Federalism* 32 (3): 89–114. http://dx.doi.org/10.1093/oxfordjournals.pubjof.a004961.

Wilkins, David E., and K. Tsianina Lomawaima. 2001. *Uneven Ground: American Indian Sovereignty and Federal Law*. Norman: University of Oklahoma Press.

Wilkins, Kerry. 2004. "Conclusion: Judicial Aesthetics and Aboriginal Claims." In *Advancing Aboriginal Claims: Visions/Strategies/Directions*, ed. Kerry Wilkins, 288–312. Saskatoon: Purich Publishing.

Williams, Robert A. 1997. *Linking Arms Together: American Indian Treaty Visions of Law and Peace, 1600–1800*. New York: Oxford University Press.

Wood, Patricia K. 2003. "Aboriginal/Indigenous Citizenship: An Introduction." *Citizenship Studies* 7 (4): 371–78. http://dx.doi.org/10.1080/136210203200013 4930.

Legislation and Jurisprudence

Bill C-31, An Act to Amend the Indian Act, R.S.C., 1985 (1st Supp.), c. 32.

Calder et al. v. Attorney-General of British Columbia [1973], S.C.R. 313 [*Calder*].

Constitution Act, 1982, being Schedule B to the *Canada Act 1982* (UK), 1982, c. 11.

C.P. v. Matsqui Indian Band, [1995] 1S.C.R. 3 [*Matsqui Indian Band*].

Delgamuukw v. British Columbia, [1997] 3 S.C.R. 1010 [*Delgamuukw*].

Guerin v. R, [1984], 2 S.C.R. 335.

Haida Nation v. British Columbia (Minister of Forests), [2004] 3 S.C.R. 511, 2004 SCC 73 [*Haida Nation*].

Lovelace v. Ontario, [2000] 1 S.C.R. 950 [*Lovelace*].

Mikisew Cree First Nation v. Canada (Minister of Heritage), [2005] 3 S.C.R. 388, 2005 SCC 69 [*Mikisew Cree*].

Mitchell v. M.N.R., [2001] 1 S.C.R. 911, 2001 SCC 33 [*Mitchell*].

Rio Tinto Alcan Inc. v. Carrier Sekani Tribal Council, [2010] 2 S.C.R. SCC 43 [*Rio Tinto*].

R. v. Adams, [1996] 3 S.C.R. 101.

R. v. Badger, [1996] 1 S.C.R. 771.

R. v. Gladstone, [1996] 2 S.C.R. 723 [*Gladstone*].

R. v. Horseman, (1990), 1 S.C.R. 901 (S.C.C.) [*Horseman*].

R. v. Marshall, [1993] 3 S.C.R. 533.

R. v. Marshall; R. v. Bernard, [2005] 2 S.C.R. 220, 2005 SCC 43 [*Marshall; Bernard*].

R. v. Pamajewon, [1996] 2 S.C.R. 821 [*Pamajewon*].

R. v. Powley, [2003] 2 S.C.R. 207, 2003 SCC 43 [*Powley*].

R. v. Sappier; R. v. Gray, [2006] 2 S.C.R. 686, 2006 SCC 54 [*Sappier; Gray*].

R. v. Sheppard, [2002] 1 S.C.R. 869, 2002 SCC 26.

R. v. Sioui, [1990] 1 S.C.R. 1025.

R. v. Sparrow, [1990] 1 S.C.R. 1075 [*Sparrow*].

R. v. Van der Peet, [1996] 2 S.C.R. 507 [*Van der Peet*].

Sawridge Band v. Canada, [1996] 1 F.C. 3 (F.C.T.D.).

Sawridge Band v. Canada, [1997] 3 F.C. 580 (F.C.A.).

Sawridge Band v. Canada, (1999) 164 F.T.R. 95 (F.C.T.D.). http://decisions.fct-cf. gc.ca/en/1999/t-66-86_1825/t-66-86.html.

Sawridge Band v. Canada, [2003] 3 C.N.L.R. 344 (F.C.T.D.).

Sawridge Band v. Canada, [2003] F.C. 1083 (F.C.T.D.). http://decisions.fct-ct.gc.ca/ en/2003/2003fc1083/2003fc1083.htmlQ12.

Sawridge First Nation v. Canada, 2009 FCA 123 (F.C.A.). http://decisions.fca-caf. gc.ca/en/2009/2009fca123/2009fca123.html.

St. Ann's Island Hunting And Fishing Club Ltd. v. R., [1950] S.C.R. 211.

St. Catherine's Lumber & Milling Co. v. The Queen, [1888], 14 App. Cas. 46 (J.C.P.C.).

Taku River Tlingit First Nation v. British Columbia (Project Assessment Director), [2004] 3 S.C.R. 550, 2004 SCC 74 [*Taku River*].

Tsilhqot'in Nation v. British Columbia, [2014] SCC 44 [*Tsilhqot'in*].

Index

aboriginality (concept): about, 9–10, 12, 32–33; academic commentary, 32, 34–35, 50; analytical and real-world costs of theories, 46–48; conceptions of the good, 37, 71–73, 75; connection to rights, 9–10, 22, 32–33, 124–25; as contested phenomenon, 33, 34–35; outsider definitions of, 48, 50; pre-contact cultures and rights, 22–26, 24–26; purpose of s. 35 as protection of, 21–23, 31–33; relational approaches, 12, 34–35, 41–45, 58–59, 82; rights and intra-group harm, 118; terminology, 10–11; traits-based approaches, 12, 34–35, 44–45. *See also* relational approaches; traits-based approaches

aboriginality (concept), definition by Aboriginal people. *See* self-definition

aboriginality (concept), definition by non-Aboriginal people: about, 76–79; analytical costs of relational approaches, 48, 50; *Delgamuukw*, 78–79; *Gladstone*, 77–78; historical background, 53; *Pamajewon*, 78; SCC submissions by Crown, 76–79; *Sparrow*, 76–77; *Van der Peet*, 77–78

Aboriginal peoples: academic commentary on, 32, 37, 94–95, 102, 104–5; associative and natural duties, 37–39; pan-Indian commonality, 37–39; pre-contact cultures and rights, 22–26, 84–85, 102, 104–5; SCC and social change, 103–5; societal culture, 5, 127*n*3; terminology, 10–11; and territory, 87; values of respect, balance, and harmony, 37, 39; worldview, 71–72. *See also* natural world; self-determination; territory and territorial claims

Aboriginal rights: about, 6–7, 20–23, 123–25; activity-based claims, 22–27, 31–33; conferences to redefine rights, proposal, 118; connection to aboriginality, 9–10, 22, 32–33, 124–25; debates on, 123–25; first ministers' conferences on s. 35,

normalization, 51–52; and power relations, 51–52, 53–56; and social exclusion, 51–52, 54–56

traits-based approaches, constitutive elements: about, 34–35, 34–41; Aboriginal attachment to land, 36–37, 39–41; associative duties, 37–39; combinations, 41; conceptions of the good, 37, 71–73; descent, 36, 39, 41; kinship relationships, 41; pan-Indian commonality, 37–38; relations to time and space, 36, 39, 41; shared cultural, spiritual, and political practices, 36, 37, 39, 41; traits-based vs relational approaches, 34–35; values of respect, balance, and harmony, 37, 39, 41

treaties and treaty rights: about, 20, 74–75; Aboriginal vs treaty rights, 20; activity-based rights, 26; constitutive elements of aboriginality, 76; nation-to-nation approach, 61, 75; *Pamajewon*, 75–76; pre-1982 debates on rights, 14; SCC submissions by Aboriginal people, 73, 74–75; and self-government, 73, 74–75, 76; source in documents, 20; *Sparrow*, 75–76; surrender of rights, 26; treaty federalism, 67, 132*n*3

trusts and fiduciary relationships, 27

Tsilhqot'in Nation v. British Columbia, 28–30, 130*n*38

Tully, James, 34–35, 61, 115–16

Turner, Dale, 11, 14, 67, 123

Turpel, Mary Ellen, 38–39, 61–62, 101

unfairness: about, 114; citizen-state approach, 13, 109, 112–18, 124–25; colonial approach, 116; Crown sovereignty, 114–16, 124–25; and justice, 114–18; self-government, 117–18; territory and territorial claims, 114–16, 124–25. *See also* moral issues

usufructary rights, 14–15, 81

Van der Peet, R. v.: about, 22–24, 70–71; academic commentary, 32, 94–95, 106–7; activity-based claims, 23–24, 131*n*51; conceptions of the good, 71–73; Crown sovereignty, 86–87; fishing, 32, 70–71, 72, 77; goal of reconciliation, 120–21; judicial decision, 83, 84–85, 86–87, 120–21; pre-contact cultures and rights, 22–23, 84–85; SCC submissions by Aboriginal people, 70–71; SCC submissions by Crown, 77; self-government rights, 106–7; "way-of-life-rights," 94

Vermette, D'Arcy, 53, 115

Waldron, Jeremy, 4

Walkem, Ardith, 114–15, 116

Watson, Ron, 51

Weinstock, Daniel, 52

Westbank First Nation (WFN), 74

Wet'suwet'en, 71–73, 78–79. See also *Delgamuukw v. British Columbia*

White Bear First Nations (WBFN), 74

Wilkins, David E., 62

Williams, Robert, 60

women: *Bill C-31* and traits-based approaches, 55–56; contracts and real-world costs, 47, 131*n*1

LAW AND
SOCIETY

Amanda Nettelbeck, Russell Smandych, Louis A. Knafla, and Robert Foster
Fragile Settlements: Aboriginal Peoples, Law, and Resistance in South-West Australia and Prairie Canada (2016)

Adam Dodek and Alice Woolley (eds.) *In Search of the Ethical Lawyer: Stories from the Canadian Legal Profession* (2016)

David R. Boyd *Cleaner, Greener, Healthier: A Prescription for Stronger Canadian Environmental Laws and Policies* (2015)

Margaret E. Beare, Nathalie Des Rosiers, and Abby Deshman (eds.) *Putting the State on Trial: The Policing of Protest during the G20 Summit* (2015)

Dale Brawn *Paths to the Bench: The Judicial Appointment Process in Manitoba, 1870–1950* (2014)

Dominique Clément *Equality Deferred: Sex Discrimination and British Columbia's Human Rights State, 1953–84* (2014)

Irvin Studin *The Strategic Constitution: Understanding Canadian Power in the World* (2014)

Elizabeth A. Sheehy *Defending Battered Women on Trial: Lessons from the Transcripts* (2014)

Carmela Murdocca *To Right Historical Wrongs: Race, Gender, and Sentencing in Canada* (2013)

Donn Short *"Don't Be So Gay!" Queers, Bullying, and Making Schools Safe* (2013)